BE A

GOOD MAN

NOT A

~~NICE GUY~~

A Guide to True Masculinity

PRAISE FOR KELVIN DAVIS'S
NOTORIOUSLY DAPPER

"Out of everyone, we're most in love with Kelvin Davis of Notoriously Dapper."

—*Glamour Magazine*

"Body positivity and some welcome diversity."

—*Cosmopolitan*

"Davis certainly has something to say to young men about what we lose when we give up the concept of being a gentleman, and what we have to gain when we cherish it."

—*The New York Times*

ALSO BY KELVIN DAVIS

Notoriously Dapper

BE A
GOOD
MAN
NOT A
~~NICE GUY~~

A Guide to True Masculinity

KELVIN DAVIS

Turner Publishing Company
Nashville, Tennessee
www.turnerpublishing.com

Be A Good Man, Not A Nice Guy: A Guide to True Masculinity
Copyright © 2026 by Kelvin Davis. All rights reserved.

This book or any part thereof may not be reproduced or transmitted in any form or by any means, electronic or mechanical, including photocopying, recording, or by any information storage and retrieval system, without permission in writing from the publisher.

Limit of Liability/Disclaimer of Warranty: While the publisher and the author have used their best efforts in preparing this book, they make no representations or warranties with respect to the accuracy or completeness of the contents of this book and specifically disclaim any implied warranties of merchantability or fitness for a particular purpose. No warranty may be created or extended by sales representatives or written sales materials. The advice and strategies contained herein may not be suitable for your situation. You should consult with a professional where appropriate. Neither the publisher nor the author shall be liable for any loss of profit or any other commercial damages, including but not limited to special, incidental, consequential, or other damages.

Scripture quotation marked (NIV) taken from the Holy Bible, New International Version®, NIV®. Copyright © 1973, 1978, 1984, 2011 by Biblica, Inc.® Used by permission of Zondervan. All rights reserved worldwide. www.zondervan.com. The "NIV" and "New International Version" are trademarks registered in the United States Patent and Trademark Office by Biblica, Inc.®

Scripture quotations marked (NKJV) are taken from the NEW KING JAMES VERSION®. Copyright© 1982 by Thomas Nelson, Inc. Used by permission. All rights reserved.

Cover and book design by William Ruoto

Library of Congress Cataloging-in-Publication Data
Names: Davis, Kelvin, 1987- author
Title: Be a good man, not a nice guy : a guide to true masculinity / Kelvin Davis.
Description: Nashville : TMA Press, [2025]
Identifiers: LCCN 2025001962 (print) | LCCN 2025001963 (ebook) | ISBN 9798887981055 paperback | ISBN 9798887981062 hardcover | ISBN 9798887981079 epub
Subjects: LCSH: Masculinity | Men—Identity | Men—Conduct of life
Classification: LCC HQ1090 .D397 2025 (print) | LCC HQ1090 (ebook) | DDC 155.3/32—dc23/eng/20250614
LC record available at https://lccn.loc.gov/2025001962
LC ebook record available at https://lccn.loc.gov/2025001963

Printed in the United States of America

This book is dedicated to my parents, Kelvin and Sharon Davis. May this book bless young boys and men everywhere, changing them from nice guys to good men. May they be guided in the right direction the same way you have led me.

TABLE OF CONTENTS

Introduction / **1**

Good Man: Security, Safety, and Sanity / **7**

Chapter 1: Nice Guy, Bad Marriage / **21**
Chapter 2: Self-Control and Confidence / **33**
Chapter 3: Learn from Losses / **41**

Good Man: Education, Environment, and Empathy / **47**

Chapter 4: You're the Problem / **59**
Chapter 5: Know Means No / **67**
Chapter 6: Good Men Do Good Shit / **75**

Three Currencies of Life: Time, Money, and Health / **82**

Good Man: Providing, Protecting, and Patience / **93**

Chapter 7: Iron Sharpens Iron / **109**
Chapter 8: Nice Guys Finish Last / **117**
Chapter 9: Frustrated Father / **127**

Good Man: Habits, Hobbies, and Happiness / **137**

CONTENTS

Chapter 10: Go to Health **/ 147**
Chapter 11: Good Man, Great Marriage **/ 157**
Chapter 12: Faith over Fear **/ 165**

Forgiven Not Forsaken: A Letter to My Mom and Dad **/ 173**

Acknowledgments **/ 179**
About the Author **/ 181**
Endnotes **/ 183**

BE A
GOOD
MAN
NOT A
~~NICE GUY~~

A Guide to True Masculinity

INTRODUCTION

I'M KELVIN DAVIS. MANY OF YOU MAY KNOW ME from my blog, *Notoriously Dapper,* Instagram, or for being the face of brands like Target and GAP. Or you may have read my first book, *Notoriously Dapper: How to Be a Modern Gentleman with Manners, Style and Body Confidence.* That book is still going strong; it was nominated for the 2018 NAACP Image Awards in the category of Most Outstanding Literary Work. Although I didn't take home the win, the experience of being an award-nominated author is pretty exhilarating to say the least. But whether you know me or not, I'm here to help you. Yes, that's correct: *help you.* The truth is, we live in a world where there are too many nice guys and not enough good men. I know what you're thinking: What's wrong with being a "nice guy"? I'm here to tell you a lot is wrong with being a nice guy. There's a reason for the saying "nice guys finish last." They often do. Trust me, I would know because I used to be a nice guy.

Let's just get straight into it. What is a nice guy? A nice guy is often a people pleaser. He will go out of his way to do things for people, but also expects something in return. That may be compensation through verbal praise or even physical touch for how great he is. He will often go against his morals and beliefs to portray an image of being a nice guy. This is the kind of guy who is married but will shamelessly cross the line with another woman who is showing interest in him instead of simply rejecting her flirtatious advances. He does this because he doesn't want to come off as "mean." He goes against his morals of respect and loyalty, acting like a nice guy to feed his ego so she doesn't say anything bad about him. You know the deal: doing things only for verbal praise.

A nice guy can often be considered "two-faced"; he hides behind a false persona of who he is to please his community of people. He will be extremely nice to colleagues, strangers, and people who work in the service industry (such as waitstaff, customer service, and maintenance workers) but will be the opposite toward his family when he arrives home. He's short with his spouse, gives limited attention to his kids, and isolates himself from taking accountability. Now, don't get me wrong, we all need that "whoosah" moment after a long day of work. That mental break is sometimes necessary after being "on" all day long. So, let's be clear: There's a difference between giving strangers grace, kindness, and understanding but not extending that same energy to your family. A nice guy will compliment someone on their appearance but won't extend that same compliment to his spouse. A nice guy will be understanding of the misbehaving toddler next to him at the restaurant but will scrutinize his own children for doing the same. You understand what I'm saying? There's a lot of "it's cool when other people do it, but it's a problem when it's my family doing it" type of energy—lots of hypocrisy within their bubble.

Nice guys will offer a homeless person a five-dollar bill while recording their good deed using their thousand-dollar phone, just to show the world how great they are and how much people should love them. While this act is generous, we must ask ourselves: Would someone be doing this if there weren't cameras around? Would you still give the homeless person money if no one saw it? What if there were no way to document your good deeds...would you still do them? If you're pondering the question or even debating internally an answer, then you are a nice guy.

While nice guys and good men often perform the same acts of kindness or gentlemanly gestures, the intent behind them is what separates the two. A good man is confident in who he is; he doesn't need verbal praise nor attention from others to satisfy his ego. He's poised and stoic but also loving, vigilant, and, most importantly, HIM. Yes, HIM! Himothy, Himmy Neutron, Himmy Hendrix; capital H, capital I, capital M... HIM. Being "HIM" is a term that solidifies the confidence in who you are as a man. A good man is secure in who he is, what he is not, and what he is capable of. A nice guy *thinks* he's HIM, but he needs the validation from others to feel that. A good man stands on what he believes in and doesn't falter because someone disagrees or disapproves. In return, this can lead to estranged relationships or even some fallouts. These actions are sometimes simply considered "the trash taking itself out." We live in a world where people from all walks of life have a different opinion about many topics. If you as an adult can't accept this without having a feud or conflict, then it's time for you to grow up. A nice guy will talk about your difference of opinion as a personal attack. He will often hold it against you in future arguments or disagreements. A good man will respect your opposite opinion without degrading or bashing you personally.

Operating as a good man does come at a cost. Like the old saying goes, "You gotta pay the cost to be the boss." That cost is often a small circle with big responsibilities. In return, a good man knows what's good for himself, his family, and those around him. He constantly builds people up, he takes initiative, and he leads with great insight. We all know some good men. We also know they can be very misunderstood. Others will take their words out of context, not realizing that a good man has no ill intent to harm anyone. He wants everyone to be safe and secure. He will not only provide rules and regulations to ensure this, but he will also enforce these rules, holding people accountable so they can also be great.

Everyone wants the good man as their boss, husband, friend, and leader, but they often forget that this comes with a man who takes charge, challenges others to be their best selves, and leads by example. Being a good man is not for the weak. It's only for the strong, the ones who are willing to be in the thick of it all. The guy who knows how daily decisions can shape his life, for better or worse. He moves with a purpose; his life is a legacy, and his family is his fortune. He's a protector, a provider, a lover, a fighter, but never a hater nor instigator. "He doesn't want a problem but if you want a problem then he says no problem." These are words by Grammy-winning rapper, actor, and producer Mr. Curtis Jackson, aka 50 Cent.

A nice guy is honest; a good man is transparent. A nice guy wants instant gratification; a good man knows the power in delayed gratification. A nice guy finds a problem; a good man finds a solution. A nice guy is controlled by his vices; a good man is controlled by his morals. A nice guy says thank you; a good man shows gratitude. A nice guy tells you a beautiful lie;

a good man tells you the ugly truth. A nice guy says he cares; a good man shows empathy. A nice guy is nice for the praise; a good man is kind with a purpose.

Now that we have established what a nice guy is and what a good man is, it's time to get into some real personal stories, where I'll share lessons I have learned, things I wish I would have done differently, and most importantly, people I wish I would have treated better. A lot has changed since my first book, which was released in 2017. I'm no longer married, and my views about it have changed drastically. While my first book was written when I was a full-time art teacher, football coach, and aspiring fashion icon, the new moments in my life since then have helped shape me into being the good man I am today. Don't get me wrong, my first book gives solid advice about being a modern gentleman, and I will reiterate most of those things in this book. But let me be clear: It is the intention behind your actions that is the difference between being a nice guy and being a good man.

I have grown a lot in the past few years. COVID-19 changed the entire world and how we operate in it. It has changed the way teachers teach, the way students learn, and how we as humans perceive the world. Yes, I got a COVID divorce; a lot of people broke up or ended marriages during that difficult time. Let's be real: It's hard being locked up in the same house with someone for that amount of time with zero breaks. Most of us were going stir-crazy in our own right. Cabin fever was itching us all over the world. I say this because if you're the same person after the COVID-19 pandemic, then you must have truly found yourself way before it started. If that's the case, then good for you, but the majority of us discovered things we didn't like about ourselves and other people. Don't feel bad about it; we are supposed to grow and ascend in this life. The journey to becoming a good man can be very daunting, especially if you're currently a nice guy. For me, realizing I was a nice guy and actively trying to change it was very difficult. And it still is at times. No one, no matter who they are or where they come from, wants to admit they have a problem. Trust me, I get it. I didn't want to admit I had problems either.

This book is going to help you do just that. You are going to learn from my experiences and stories. We all have things to say, and we all have a reason to say them. I have a good bit to say, my reason for saying it being *we need more good men*. We currently live in a world where they rarely exist. Not only will you be able to become a good man, but you will be able to spot one as well. You can build a solid group of good men to keep you company. Good men who raise great children for this society we live in. It will be a great generational gift to pass on and on through your family. On top of that, you are helping mold a new generation of children who will eventually run this world. I don't know about you, but I'm tired of racism, homophobia, anti-feminism, and overall hate. We can do better. We can *be* better.

Alright, alright. I've rambled on enough in this introduction. Now it's time to rumble. Let's get this shit started. Welcome to *Be a Good Man, Not a Nice Guy*.

Good Man: Security, Safety, and Sanity

Solid foundational character traits help build you as a man. Think of it as the foundation to your house. If you have a bad foundation, the chances of your house crumbling under any troubling circumstance are very high. On the other hand, if your house has a solid foundation, it can more easily withstand any negative impact. Houses with solid foundations also have more value, they are trusted more, and they provide a sense of safety and security for the individuals living there. Just like everyone wants a house with a solid foundation, everyone wants a man with solid foundational character traits.

Many nice guys lack certain foundational character traits. In these "Good Man" sections, we will dive deep into the characteristics I think are vital for a good man to possess. In this first section, we will address security, safety, and sanity. These three terms can be applied to your life in various ways. As we delve more into these, I will share personal experiences along with solutions to circumstances you can actively use in real time. Remember, we have a variety of currencies in this life; time, money, and health are just a few of them. As you continue to go through this journey, understand that being a good man comes at a cost. The question is: Are you willing to pay the amount to achieve it?

SECURITY

Most of us think of security as a form of protection for others and ourselves. While that is true in many cases, I also want to speak on how security in yourself is needed to be a well-rounded person in life. You see, a lot of men take out their insecurities on other people. Whether it be in friendships, relationships, or work-related partnerships, we can often project our insecurities onto other people without even noticing it. This can manifest as having trust issues because of past experiences, so in return you project the insecurity of assuming someone is lying to you when they are in fact being truthful. I personally have assumed negative intent when something happens due to having people in my life do things to me with the intention of being hurtful. Because of this I have had moments where instead of giving grace and assuming positive intent, I have assumed the worst and have dished out consequences to people who really didn't mean me any harm. Many refer to this behavior as self-sabotaging; I considerate it a trauma response. We have all encountered a situation that has made us feel some sort of shame or embarrassment, and these moments can cause us to develop an insecurity. It's important not to let these insecurities get the best of us.

Securities and insecurities come in a variety of facets, from physical or emotional to financial or mental. One of the most common insecurities we face in society is related to body image. The media often puts an unrealistic expectation on how we should look. Believe it or not, this affects men and how we move day to day. Most men in general will never admit they have body image insecurity because it is often stigmatized as a predominantly female issue. But the reality is, it affects everyone of all ages, races, and genders.

Many people take this insecurity out on themselves and others, but it can look different in many areas of life, one of them being how you perform when you have a task to complete. For instance, when I was a middle school head football coach years ago, we would occasionally play schools whose programs were better funded. Where the money came from, I don't know, and neither did I care. But when you have more money, you tend to have access to better workout facilities, food, and so on. Unfortunately, our school didn't have a lot of funds; we didn't have access to a weight room, decent uniforms, or equipment. As the head coach, I did the best I could with what I had, but nothing could stop my team from feeling insecure when they saw the other team show up. I remember it like it was yesterday: We were heading out to play one of our rival schools, one that had better uniforms and that some would say on paper were the better team.

Although my team was secure, confident, and hyped about playing and winning this game when we arrived, that all changed when we stepped on the field. Because the other team looked more put together uniform-wise, it drove an instant insecurity within my team. They started talking about how awesome the opposing team looked and started questioning why they didn't have uniforms that looked more aesthetically pleasing. Instead of being focused on our game plan and how we were going to execute it, they were too preoccupied that the opposing team was better because of how they looked. The great Deion Sanders, Hall of Fame football player and now head coach, said it best: "If you look good, you feel good. If you feel good, you play good. If you play good, they pay good." This couldn't have been truer for us. We tried our best by running what we practiced and playing our game, but the team's insecurities about how they looked won out, and unfortunately, we lost the game 38–0.

In life, hard work always beats talent, especially when talent doesn't work hard. But we can often psych ourselves out by overthinking scenarios in our head, and this is exactly what happened to my team. During the postgame speech, I spoke to them about how important it is to be confident with yourself, your abilities, and your talent but to also be secure in yourself and the game plan. Their lack of security defeated the confidence they had prior to the game, and they came up short. Seeing this unfold let me know we had to work more on building up their resilience as a team.

When secure within, we are able to properly provide safety for ourselves and those around us. For instance, if my quarterback is secure in himself, the game plan, and his talents, then the rest of the offense is going to be secure as well. As a coach, that makes me feel safe in our ability to execute what we have practiced. Sometimes it takes a leader to demonstrate that initial security in order for others to feel it as well. We can apply this method to any part of our lives. In the workplace, we trust a secure boss to lead us to greatness. When they are insecure, it also makes the employees insecure. When we are insecure, we become unsure, which can translate to indecisiveness, lack of safety, and overall chaos.

Security in any form is necessary to foster positive relationships in our lives. When people feel secure around you, they can often be themselves and feel safe around you. This goes for work, parenting, relationships, and friendships. My daughters can 100 percent be themselves around me because I provide a secure and safe space for them to do so. They can talk to me about problems they have without me trying to shame them, get upset with them, or invalidate how they feel. The easiest way to get someone to stop coming to you is to make them feel insecure and unsafe around you. No one wants to be that guy who is so insecure within himself that he projects it on to others. As a man, you have to fix that so you can prosper, nurture, and build relationships with people in your life. Being a good man means being a secure space for people and yourself.

SAFETY

Being a safe space means you are enforcing boundaries and rules. Rules keep us in line as a society. We follow rules every day and don't even think about them. When driving, we stop at red lights, go on green lights, use our signals to turn, and obey traffic laws. If we don't follow those rules and boundaries, there are consequences, whether that be a car accident or getting a ticket. The main point of this is that law and order have to be established for people to feel safe. We avoid places that are unsafe but are drawn to places and people that make us feel safe and protected. Safe spaces are vital. A good man will provide safety at his work, in his relationship, with his kids, and with his friends, but this is something nice guys have trouble doing. Oftentimes nice guys want to avoid accountability or anything that questions who they truly are. They will do this by being evasive during certain interactions with others; they will act sheepish and not want to take criticism to ensure a better outcome. This type of behavior can lead others to feel unsafe around you. If you can't use discernment and change who you are to better yourself then you're losing the game of life. Most people feel safe around those who can take accountability for their actions. Granted, we all make mistakes in life, but imagine having to constantly be around a person that does things that hurt you but never takes responsibility for it, let alone change their behavior. It's natural to begin to withdraw from them because you feel unsafe. You can't trust them to do the right thing.

When we have a job, we want the good man—not the nice guy—to be the boss. Good men often hold people accountable while also taking responsibility. They demand people to fall in line with the standards they have set. For instance, if an employee is late to work, they don't get a pass simply because they are a "good" employee or they have a better rapport with the boss. They get the same reprimand as anyone else that would show up late to work. But a nice guy as a boss will play a game of favorites by picking and choosing from his own merit who deserves punishment for being late. Doing this creates an insincere work environment where employees feel like they have to compete to be the favorite in order to avoid accountability, rather than creating an environment that requires them to follow a standard work ethic. Not being equally fair is how you lose the trust and respect of your employees. In the words of former head football coach Nick Saban, "Everyone has to buy into your standards of greatness in order to be successful as a group. High achievers don't like mediocre people, and mediocre people don't like high achievers." You can apply this to every aspect of your life but especially when it comes to your career.

We touched on safety briefly when discussing the benefits of being secure within yourself and how it can affect your actions and responses to certain situations in life. While *security* and *safety* are similar terms, they are very different. Many like to think of security as a measure of protection in case something happens, while safety is a boundary or provision put into place to prevent something from happening.

Physical safety is just as important as emotional safety, especially as a father. Your children have to know that you are the one who will protect them at all costs. All men are built differently and that's understandable, but every man should have some sort of ability to protect himself and his family. You have to be able to stand on business in times of danger. If you're able-bodied, you need to be going to the gym regularly to build strength and stamina. This has nothing to do with the way you need to look but everything to do with how you can provide physical safety for others and for yourself. God forbid you ever have to put your life on the line to protect your family, but if you do, you want to be able to do that with confidence and security. Strength training through lifting weights and cardio can give you the security to provide that physical safety when it's needed. By doing this, you are also becoming the healthiest version of yourself. In return, the investment will not only be physical safety for your family but you will be providing security for your family by living longer as well.

Women love feeling safe; if you want a woman to trust you, then you must provide safety for her—safety in your ability to help her when she needs it, safety in listening to her, and safety in her ability to be herself. Nice guys have trouble with women because they are disingenuous in their pursuits. Everything feels like a game, and they have the tendency to make people feel like they must give something in return for a good deed. A good man is the man who comes off so genuine that a woman doesn't have to question if he has ulterior motives. A nice guy will not only make a woman question it, but he will make her feel so unsure that she will not be able to be her full self around him. There's a saying that goes around on social media: "Masculine men raise feminine women, and feminine men raise masculine women." Now, a lot of this can be taken out of context and used in a verbal battlefield to prove points that don't even need to be proven. The fact is that men are typically more logical, and women are typically more emotional. Please understand that this is a generality—of course there are some exceptions. We have all encountered some men who are more emotional and some women who are more logical. That doesn't negate from the generality of the majority. Naturally being either one of these things is not a bad thing. This is why we all need each other: Men need women and women need men. As a society, we have got to stop this mindset of men versus women and women versus men. The truth is, the dynamic of masculine and feminine energies are not only needed but they are beautiful, especially when both parties are able to embrace them properly. I feel as though that "saying" is simply relating and giving insight to how the dynamics of improperly embraced masculinity in men can throw off nature's plan when dealing with parenthood.

For instance, if you are raised by a more feminine father figure, the chances of you being more masculine is high because you have to deal with his emotional responses rather than him being logically sound. By dealing with those emotional responses, you have to become more stoic and less emotional yourself. This happens in any situation where the masculine and feminine energies meet. If a more masculine woman dates a masculine man, the probability of conflict is going to be higher. Because, subconsciously, they are both fighting for that masculine role in the relationship. But a lot of this conflict can be avoided if safe yet uncomfortable conversations are had. The problem is that many people want to avoid accountability, which makes them run from the problem instead of facing it. When we are able to have uncomfortable conversations, it can lead to having effective change. I know personally when I have dealt with masculine women in a romantic setting, I've found it's best to be stoic and let them know my masculine energy is present by not responding emotionally during conflict. You can get your point across without being aggressive, and you can handle things better when you are calm.

This is something that has to be practiced and perfected over time. Being a safe space can get exhausting at times, but it's a lot better than being the unsafe space that people avoid. When things get overwhelming and you feel like you're being "swalllllowwwed up," as American pastor and motivational speaker T. D. Jakes would say, remember that if you weren't a good man, then no one would want to be around you. Be the safe space. We need more good God-fearing men in this world, men who believe in providing security and safety. Without it, we don't have much, but with it, we have everything.

SANITY

Sanity, by definition, is the ability to think, operate, and behave in a normal or rational manner. We have all been in moments where our sanity has been compromised. Most of us have had this done through gaslighting. Many people misuse and overuse this term daily, but it is, in fact, something serious that people encounter. Gaslighting is a form of manipulation where someone convinces you that your reality is false, and, if done effectively, it can violate your sanity. This may happen when someone has said something, you call them out on it, and they then tell you they never said that. They convince you so much of their truth that you forget your own reality. It can make you feel a bit insane. This is why it's important to protect your sanity, or as some would say "protect your peace."

Situations that compromise your sanity need to be avoided at all costs. Having the awareness to notice it's happening along with having the emotional intelligence to escape it can help protect your peace. Be vigilant about who you let close to you; the enemy loves to go for your head and heart. If others can make you think certain things in your head and believe it in your heart, then they have power over you. It's important to be aware of people's intentions and pay close attention to how they treat you.

My pastor made a reference to this once during Bible study. He related it to when we are in battle and the enemy goes for one of two kill shots: one to annihilate the target by aiming for their head, or one aiming for the heart. While this is true for the physical part of battle, this is also true for spiritual warfare as well. Allowing access to your head and heart puts you in a vulnerable place. That's why choosing what you watch, read, and listen to can play a role in your reality. We live in a time where people, especially kids, are becoming less compassionate for the human race because they are so disconnected from interacting with others. They are too busy catching the newest social media trend to focus on human connection. I'm a millennial, and I feel fortunate enough to have grown up with some technology but also played outside a lot with my friends. There was a nice balance to it. Just like everything in life, we need balance to keep us stable and content. Limiting our reliance on technology helps lower the obsession and addiction we have with social media and our tendencies to use it to escape reality.

But we can't blame technology for the misdirection of our kids. We as adults have to take accountability with what we allow them to have access to. Explain to them why it's important to have balance. I tell my daughters all the time that algorithms work both ways in life. Just like how social media apps have their own algorithms and show us more of what we are interested in, life does the same. The entire universe also has its own algorithm and it shows us more of what we're thinking, feeling, and focusing on. This is why we have to be careful of what and how much we consume online and offline. Even adults can get too occupied with doomscrolling after a long day of work. Using that accountability as an example can help maintain the balance we may lack. Because our hearts and minds can be so easily targeted with social media, it's important not to indulge in such negativity. There's good and bad that comes with social media, but the truth is there has been more good to come out of it than bad in the way it can foster connections among people. For example, I probably wouldn't have the platform to write this book if it wasn't for social media. We also have been graced with countless wholesome, viral moments that have restored our faith in humanity.

Surrounding yourself with positivity fuels your sanity. It allows you to operate under a sound sense of mental health. "Taking care of our mentals," as my favorite running back Marshawn Lynch would say, is a top priority. We focus so much on exercising our bodies, but we don't do the same for our minds. To be a completely balanced person, we have to focus on the physical and the mental. We must exercise our minds as much as our bodies. The beauty of it is that when we move our bodies, it helps with releasing stress from our minds. Having activities we can regularly do to release serotonin helps with enhancing our sanity.

My grandma used to tell me that "an idle mind is the devil's workshop," and she's right. When our mind is idle, we tend to lean into dark moments, forgetting to focus on the light. We overthink or get caught up in the past, and we often go down this spiral of rumination, which leads us to a mentally unhealthy state. That is why you have to protect your sanity by doing what's best for you, being secure with yourself, having safe places—and being a safe place for others—and surrounding yourself with positivity. Security, safety, and sanity—these three characteristics are essential to becoming a good man. You need all three of them, and you must use them in your life. No one is perfect, and it's okay if you make mistakes. Give yourself grace and continue to do better daily.

CHAPTER 1:

NICE GUY, BAD MARRIAGE

WE LIVE IN A TIME WHERE ABOUT 50 PERCENT of marriages don't make it. I have become part of that statistic. Divorce is so emotionally and mentally draining. You literally watch someone you've known, perhaps for years, become a stranger, to an extent. It's a situation that brings out the worst in us, especially when there is the added conflict of child custody, money, or assets. I know I'm not the first guy to fight for their rights as a father, and I won't be the last, but that doesn't make the situation any easier to deal with. The litigation can not only run you into a financial grave, but it can also alter the way you view romantic relationships going forward. The emotional turmoil of a hostile litigation can often feel like a terrorist negotiation. You go back and forth constantly about this and that; it can feel like it's never ending.

When I was married, I did the bare minimum to try to keep my marriage afloat and often did things I am not proud of. I was the definition of a nice guy. But just because you do nice things, doesn't always mean they are good things. In other words: Not all good things are nice. What do I mean by that? Oftentimes doing a *good* thing isn't a *nice* thing. For instance, when I started to gain online notoriety for my platform, I would often get flirty DMs from women. Instead of doing the good thing, which is ignoring them or even shutting down their sexually suggestive behavior, I reciprocated the flirtation. Although a part of this was ego driven, another part of it was trying to maintain a "nice guy" image by responding to them. As a good man, I now recognize that was distasteful behavior. One of the main things about this transition from a nice guy to a good man is forgiving yourself for your past and understanding that you are not your past mistakes. Of course, if I had the ability to go back in time, I would have done things differently in many ways, but we can't do that. What's happened has happened, and there's nothing I can do about it now.

Marriages end for various reasons: Some people grow apart, some people have affairs, some of it is financially driven, or even family feuds can cause a wedge between you and your spouse. Like a lot of spouses, I had an estranged relationship with my mother-in-law for many reasons. This was one of the driving forces of my divorce. While this sort of thing isn't unique nor uncommon in many marriages, from my own personal experience I have found that it's the spouse's responsibility not to allow any type of disrespect by any family member on their side. Especially if the disrespect is unwarranted or due to your race, religion, or cultural background. Unfortunately, I was the recipient of some disrespectful behavior on numerous occasions during my marriage.

Although I can recall many of these events, one of the main instances happened during 2020, which was a rough year for the entire world because everything was locked down. Being quarantined for almost a year drove many people like myself into the realization that their current situation just wasn't working. The rise in the divorce rate during COVID wasn't surprising to me at all. While some people used it as time to get closer with their spouse, a lot of us found ourselves growing more distant even though we were "closer" by being in the same space 24/7. My ex-wife, who was a middle school Spanish teacher, was teaching her classes virtually during the COVID lockdown. Since my schedule was very flexible due to my being a full-time social media influencer, I was available to help our children with all their virtual learning needs at the time.

While we were doing all this in Columbia, South Carolina, my ex-wife expressed wanting a change of scenery and asking if I wanted to go to her mom's beach house in Venice, Florida. She said, "If I'm going to have to teach kids virtually and you help the kids with their virtual work, we might as well do it from the beach," which honestly wasn't a bad idea. I also knew it would be difficult for her to teach and help the kids with their work if she went to Florida alone, especially because my youngest daughter, who is dyslexic, was just learning how to read during virtual learning and needed extra help. So, I obliged, and we decided to go for a few weeks.

When we arrived, we were greeted by my now ex-mother-in-law. During this exchange, she greeted everyone warmly with a hug and enthusiasm, but she didn't greet me with the same energy. The nice guy in me always let the actions slide because I didn't want to rock the boat. I know now as a good man that I should have addressed the behavior when it occurred to avoid frustration building inside. By addressing the behavior, I would hold her accountable and explain to her that that kind of behavior isn't acceptable, especially in front of our kids. But the nice guy in me was waiting for my wife to mention it or hold her mother accountable. What I have now realized is that you can't expect someone else to handle a situation the same way you would. If you do that, you will be disappointed every time.

The first two weeks went as smoothly as they possibly could, but I knew it was only a matter of time before her mother said something to me that would upset me or get under my skin. It didn't take long for her (a middle-aged white woman) to start having what I felt were racially-motivated microaggressions toward me, saying things like, "You're too Black to be out in the sun all day." Being a nice guy sucks because you do so much to please people, and you often end up neglecting yourself in the process. Because I wanted to keep the peace and not say what was bothering me about the tension between my mother-in-law and me for the sake of my wife, I ended up harboring all this pent-up frustration and anger, which eventually led to me having some resentment toward my wife.

Now, don't get me wrong—my ex-wife said to me numerous times that she confronted her mother about her antics toward me, but that she would always "play dumb" and say things like "I didn't mean it that way." While this could have been her truth, I personally believe that saying to your Black son-in-law that he's too Black to be out in the sun on the beach has some racist undertones, especially if you're a white lady saying it. Life experiences as a Black man have taught me that you don't have to be overly aggressive to show racism; this is why the term "microaggressions" exists. Most of the time these little aggressions are motivated by someone's differences, because of their race, culture, religion, or sexual orientation. While these actions may seem petty and are sometimes so small that it's almost unnoticeable to everyone but the recipient, they still cause an adverse reaction to the party receiving it.

Although situations like this would happen more times than I wanted them to, I would usually ignore it to avoid conflict and keep the peace for my ex-wife's sake. But there was another time I couldn't do that. My youngest daughter, Flo, was craving macaroni and cheese. She asked her grandmother (my mother-in-law) to make her some. She did, but unfortunately, it was the kind from the box, and we all know that kind isn't that good. Flo wasn't expecting that; she's used to the mac 'n' cheese my mother makes, which is that rich, delicious southern soul food mac 'n' cheese that takes at least an hour to make. You know, the kind you can cut into a square and enjoy. The look on Flo's face when she was brought the bowl of boxed mac 'n' cheese was not only hilarious, but it was priceless. It's the face every Black person makes when they see raisins in the potato salad. The look of confusion, disgust, and disappointment (if you know, you know). Flo, as politely as she could, asked what it was. My ex-mother-in-law said, "It's mac 'n' cheese, like what you asked for." I knew what was going to happen next: Flo did not want to eat it.

My ex-mother-in-law's response was not only embarrassment but anger as well, which became clear on her face when she turned red and said, "Well, I just can't do anything right."

I could tell that she possibly felt inadequate because she had come up short in satisfying Flo. And I clearly don't think it helped that what she made for Flo was being compared to my mother's way of cooking. After Flo refused to eat it, she then asked me if I could make the mac 'n' cheese that Nanny makes, "Nanny" being my mother. (From a completely biased point of view, she's the best. If you ask anyone else, including my daughters, they will agree with me times one million.) I decided to take on this task of making the mac 'n' cheese because I had time (hell, we were quarantined on a weekend with nothing to do). I called my mom to get the list of ingredients and recipe from her. I went to the store and got all the ingredients, which consisted of three different cheeses, eggs, butter, and macaroni noodles. I followed the steps and started cooking. Although Flo had to wait a little while, I was able to deliver on the request of fresh mac 'n' cheese, the Nanny way.

Somehow, I became the "bad guy" because I made my mother's mac 'n' cheese. My ex-mother-in-law made it about race, saying how the kids liked the "Black grandmother's" mac 'n' cheese more than hers. She was trying to get my ex-wife to sympathize with her, so I was happy that my ex-wife didn't engage with that nonsense. It reminded me of when a little kid acts out because they are jealous that their sibling is getting all the attention. I get it. This happens a lot, but as an adult it's a bit strange to watch it unfold with another adult. Now I know, understand, and recognize how people have unhealed traumas, and how those can show up when a person is triggered. It doesn't excuse any of those actions, but it gives the reaction an explanation. Although these reactions can be unhinged in many ways, it's important to be aware of that and how they can impact a situation. I know firsthand how reacting can cause a little situation to become a big problem. We as humans can't let our emotions get the best of us. We have to practice stoicism along with the ability to relate to the circumstance at hand. I could have done a much better job of doing this during certain interactions with my mother-in-law.

As time went on, the tension between my mother-in-law and me got worse and worse. Things went from being semi-cordial to me actively avoiding all interactions with her. I was tired of walking on eggshells and being in a hostile environment because of the tension. This is such a nice guy move, because we as nice guys often want to avoid conflict for the sake of not making trouble. But sometimes the trouble is necessary. That's why Representative John Lewis said, "get in good trouble." We as good men need to be reminded that getting into good trouble for the benefit of a positive change is not a bad thing. With this in mind, I decided to calmly confront her. I approached her while she was in the kitchen feeding her dogs and started off by saying that I wanted to know her intention behind some of the comments she made about my skin tone and bringing up the race of my mother when talking about the mac 'n' cheese. Like how most people react when they get confronted with something they did wrong, she made it into an argument instead of having a productive conversation about how she can be better and move forward. This conversation didn't go anywhere. As tensions got higher, I decided to walk away. I didn't want my anger or emotions to get the best of me. I especially didn't want my kids to see or hear me raising my voice at their grandmother. Later that evening, I told my ex-wife that I was going to leave the next day, explaining why I felt uncomfortable and why I felt the need to go. Instead of her standing up for me, leaving with me, and setting a boundary with regard to her mother's behavior and telling her it wouldn't be tolerated, she chose to stay there. Not only did she choose to stay, but she chose to make me feel bad for wanting to leave. I genuinely felt like I had no other option. Staying there under those circumstances was not in my cards. I wanted to have peace, and I wanted to make my position known that I would not be treated a certain way.

I woke up the next morning, told my kids goodbye, rented a car, and proceeded to drive back home to Columbia. The drive is over nine hours, so I had a lot of time for reflection. As I drove, I started thinking about all the times my ex-mother-in-law had been microaggressive toward me and why my ex-wife did not want to address this with me as a team. Little did I know that this would start a chain of actions and reactions that would eventually end my marriage for good. I started to develop a lack of respect for my wife. I no longer saw her as someone who was on my team. I viewed her as someone who was an opposition to me in many ways. During this time, the tragedy of George Floyd occurred, and I felt like, as a Black man, I couldn't catch a break. Not only was I directly dealing with racism within my marriage, but I was also dealing with it from the outside world. I felt like I was understood and supported by everyone except my spouse. This drove a wedge between us on so many levels that I had no desire to reconcile. I wanted out in every way possible. I wanted to be in a place where I felt loved, respected, supported, and understood. That world did not exist for me at the house I was co-habiting in, so I started to develop more online friendships with people who were inspired by what I did on my platform.

BE A GOOD MAN, NOT A NICE GUY

I also started to get close to a friend I used to work with when I was a middle school art teacher. We developed a beautiful friendship built on lighthearted fun, support, and mutual respect. This was a welcome change from what I had been experiencing. After months of barely any interaction between us, my wife and I decided to get a divorce in March 2021. I moved out in April, and I have been at peace ever since. The nice guy in me wanted to stay for my kids' sake and make sure they had both parents in the house as one unit. But the good man in me knew that seeing us as two separate healthy adults was so much better for them than living in a house filled with bad energy. Again, this is why I say being a good man often means doing things that aren't nice, and being a nice guy sometimes means you do things that aren't good.

As hard as it was, it was important for me to accept my role in the failure of our marriage. I was too much of a nice guy and failed to stand up for myself in the marriage on numerous occasions, often choosing the easy way out, which was ignoring important conversations and avoiding verbal conflict. I was so tired of arguing my point of view. Pastor Keion Henderson once said something on a viral TikTok clip: "When a man does not feel appreciated in the area of his presence, he becomes a version of a man that he can give you, and still survive. That version of him is silent, frustrated, sharp with his words…non-communicative." This is exactly what happened to me. I became silent, frustrated, sharp with my words, and very non-communicative. This version of me was my way of surviving in a situation where I just needed to get by day-to-day. We often become versions of ourselves we don't like when we are in survival mode.

After I moved out, I realized I had been acting like a nice guy in my marriage by trying to survive in a relationship that had been over for us long before COVID-19 came along. Like I mentioned earlier, quarantine caused many people to face things they'd been running from for a long time. It made me face the reality of a failing, irreconcilable marriage and the fear of having to start over, hire an attorney, go to court, pay child support, and become another statistic. Trust me when I say, all of that is worth it when you have mental peace. The hardest part of the divorce is the children; as much as you try for them not to be affected by it, they end up getting caught in the crosshairs. Luckily, my kids are a bit older, and they can read between the lines a little bit. Fortunately, they are doing great with everything now; time, therapy, and relational repair can fix a lot of wounds caused by divorce. It's important that although you don't agree with everything that happens during litigation, to keep the kids out of it and try your best to keep things positive with them.

Although I personally did not have a good marriage, the ending of it made me realize that no matter how I may feel in the moment, it's important to never make a permanent decision based on temporary emotions, which is ultimately what occurred many times during the course of my marriage. As a good man you have to take these lessons and use them to become a *better* man. Being a good man isn't about always getting it right and being perfect. It's about trying to do your best with good intentions in mind. Do we fall short? Of course we do. The important thing is to first pick yourself up and then use the lesson as a reason to do better the next time around. Nice guys tend to lack this, and they have a habit of making bad choices over and over again, which can lead to a life of misery for all involved. I have understood the importance of micro-decisions and how they can impact my life greatly. I have forgiven myself and vowed never to let it happen the second time around if I ever do decide to get married again.

In this life, we all must go through tough things to become better humans, especially during the transition to becoming a good man. No matter what you're going through in your career or relationships, or what you're feeling mentally, physically, or emotionally, you can and will come out better on the other end if you decide to make better choices. All you have to do is get through the tough times the best way you know how. Take it one day at a time. Life is not a sprint, it's a marathon, and we are all on our own journey. To be honest with you, the beauty lies in the unknown; if we knew, there would be no reason to have faith. Faith combats the fear of the unknown. We often have fear because we believe the worst is going to happen, but we can easily swap that with faith and believe that the best is going to happen. Keep faith with you at your weariest moments. God only gives his toughest battles to his strongest soldiers. As I continue to face battles throughout life, I keep the words of my father with me: "Take it chin up and chest out; it's not over till it's over. If you wake up, you've got another chance."

CHAPTER 2:

SELF-CONTROL AND CONFIDENCE

THE OLDER WE GET, THE MORE IMPORTANT IT IS to have confidence in who you are. Many men suffer from insecurities and self-confidence issues, whether it be about body image, income, or simply comparing themselves to other men. We all face it in different parts of our lives. It's no secret that I have struggled with my own body image over the years. This is due to how men are often perceived in the media and the pressure to be perceived as masculine. With men's fitness magazine covers often telling us how to get a bigger chest, more well-defined abs, and larger arms, it's easy to get lost in the sauce. We can quickly lose who we are as men by trying to become something we see on a magazine cover. Men suffer from eating disorders, mental health plights, and emotional distress trying to maintain an image created by society. That's why it's so important to develop confidence within yourself. There are many ways to help you find confidence, but understand that this takes work. You have to look in the mirror, reflect, and start the process of building who you are as a man.

The right doors won't open for you until you're the version of yourself that's meant to walk through them. Most of us want to avoid the work we need to do to become better men. We must often face the realities of our insecurities: where they come from, why we have them, and most importantly, how we overcome them. Confidence is a key attribute of a good man. Confidence is about having trust in oneself and one's abilities, and standing firm in one's beliefs. A confident man knows his worth and is not easily swayed by others' opinions. He exudes an aura of self-assurance and is not afraid to take risks or face challenges. Confidence allows a man to pursue his goals and aspirations with determination, no matter the obstacles he may face. It also makes him attractive as it shows that he is secure in himself and does not seek validation from others.

Personally, I found that building most of my self-confidence started with how well I'm able to dress. I knew from an early age that I may not always be the best-looking, the strongest, or the funniest man in the room, but I could always be the best-dressed one.

Another way to build confidence is to acknowledge what your strengths are. You might be the smartest one, the most creative one, the most empathetic one; whatever it is, own it. You were made that way for a reason. I live by the quote "Just be yourself because everyone else is taken." This is why we are all made differently. When you truly understand that, you can start to develop confidence. Find something you're good at and use that as the foundation to build your house of confidence. For instance, if you're a good artist, use that gift to propel your confidence. It makes you unique; not everyone you meet is good at art, and people will find it exciting. Your knowledge and confidence in what you are good at is going to take time to build, but when it does, you will see a difference in your ability to hold conversations and try new things.

Being a five-foot-ten bald, Black male teacher from South Carolina with aspirations of being a model and public figure in the fashion industry, I had to develop confidence. Enough that it gave me thick skin in the vastly superficial world of modeling. I started my body-positive menswear blog with the notion of helping men find confidence through dressing better. This worked for me on many levels. While I was taking pictures for my blog, I was able to work on my poses for various outfits. Unbeknownst to me, I was secretly preparing myself for becoming one of the most successful Big & Tall models in this industry. Growing up, I had parents who truly believed in me, who made me believe that I can accomplish anything. I think that's why I have little to no fear when chasing a goal. I don't mind the rejection or the failure; in fact, I welcome it. It helps me become better on the other side. I truly can't name a time when I failed and learned nothing. I always learn something, whether it be to my benefit or not. I have the mindset to keep going to see what the outcome could be if I keep trying. This is where a lot of my self-control and confidence takes over.

In the entertainment industry, you will lose jobs, money, and your mind if you let your emotions control you. Making an emotional decision will cost you every time. I can say without a shadow of a doubt, I have made emotional decisions that have impacted my life in many ways, one of them being in my relationship with my sister, whom I didn't speak to for over two years. We had a huge falling out on our last summer vacation together. I don't know if it will ever be repaired fully, but I do know that it was an emotional decision on both ends for us to act that way toward each other. I'm not here to pin the blame on anyone for things that have gone awry in my life. I want to take full responsibility and continue to grow as a man. Unfortunately, people have family feuds all the time, some of which last a few hours and some that last forever.

There are a lot of people who have lost everything they have worked so hard for just because they didn't have self-control in a situation. Self-control is the ability to regulate one's emotions, thoughts, and actions. It requires discipline, restraint, and the ability to resist temptation. A man who exhibits self-control is capable of staying calm in challenging situations and making rational decisions. This trait is especially important in relationships and interactions with others. A man who has self-control is less likely to lose his cool and react impulsively, which we know can lead to negative consequences. This quality also reflects maturity and responsibility as it shows that a man is able to take control of his own emotions and actions.

I know my self-control hasn't always been top-tier in my life. I am reminded of this when I think about the situation between my sister and me. We got into a disagreement about the way her wife had verbally disciplined one of my kids. As a concerned parent, I went to talk to her wife about it; my sister came to her defense, and things spun out of control very quickly. I don't want to dive too deep into it because we have all healed and time has helped repair that bridge. But that situation proved to me that when you have the option to walk away, just do it. Unfortunately, during that altercation, I didn't. I let my anger get the best of me, and I suffered a loss from it. This loss was the closeness of the relationship I had with my sister. If I could go back in time, I would have reacted with much more stoicism and poise. As I wonder how this will affect our relationship long-term because of my emotional rage, I am left feeling somber most days. In the words of actor and professional wrestler Dwayne "The Rock" Johnson, "we need people with more poise and less noise." These are words I try to live by, especially when I am challenged in life. Situations will arise where we must practice moving with more poise and less noise.

We as men all wrestle with our vices or demons. I have had my fair share of them; I used to be addicted to porn. Studies have shown that porn creates an unrealistic standard of intimacy. Many men seek out fantasies online and live vicariously through OnlyFans models and porn websites. Doing this makes you unproductive in many ways. Seeking that kind of satisfaction gives you a false sense of accomplishing something you didn't do. I noticed that after I watched porn, I was less motivated to do anything else. I would often be disengaged emotionally and romantically; this would cause issues in my marriage when my wife was looking for connection. This is why practicing self-control is so necessary when you are evolving into a good man. You can't keep those nice guy traits and simply get better at hiding the things you struggle with. You have to confront them and eventually defeat them. This can come in the form of therapy or your own self-reflection. Sometimes it takes both to conquer what you're struggling with. During an interview, David Goggins, retired United States Navy SEAL, author, and motivational speaker, once said, "We are all fucked up, everyone you know is fucked up. The only difference between them and you, is that they have found a way to hide it better than you do, that's all."

And he's right. While we walk around looking at everyone else's perfect life, based on what they choose to share on social media and in person, we get lost in what reality actually is. The truth is, we only share and post our highlights in life. We rarely see the full picture into someone's life, and that's the way it's meant to be. Social media is this fantasyland of people pretending to be something they are not. I'm not saying we all do this, but even for myself as a social media influencer, I get caught up in posting a perfectly curated line of posts that promote me in the most positive way.

My grandmother always told me that when you ask for something, God never gives it to you directly. Instead, he gives you situations where what you asked for is needed. For instance, if you ask God for strength, he doesn't just give it to you—he gives you an opportunity to become strong. In that situation, you will find the strength and resilience to get through the plight. Don't worry; we don't always get it right the first time. I'm sure when that argument arose between my sister and me, it was a chance for me to practice my stoicism I had been asking God for. It's moments like these when your thoughts and actions need to be in alignment. I didn't get it right that time, but understand that God makes no mistakes. Sometimes you need it to go the opposite way so you can see the severity of the outcome your actions caused. I now know as the man I am today how important it is for me to not react emotionally because it can cost me big time.

As I mentioned earlier, I try to learn from all my mistakes. Because of this I am now able to think more clearly before reacting out of emotion. You learn how to do this a lot as a father because, let's be honest, kids will test every inch of your patience. It's important to react with a clear head during times you have to discipline them. You can't let your emotions get the best of you and over-punish a child for something that is minor. I try my best to hand out punishments that match the crime. Your children are also going to have moments of frustration and anger. It's your job to approach it like a levelheaded adult. I have seen so many parents over-discipline their kids or even attack their kid's personal character over a mistake. As a father, I don't ever want to make a bad decision, especially one that's based on a temporary emotion. I take this into account not only when I'm parenting but when I'm dealing with business and my personal life. You will be amazed how one wrong outburst can change everything for the worse. You could lose a business deal, potential booking with a client, custody of your children, and more by reacting irrationally. Being able to take a step back and think before reacting can not only make the situation better but it can help you be a better man in every other aspect of your life. From personal to business, I now move with a purpose, and my priority is not getting caught up in the negatives.

One of the ways I do this is by focusing on how to turn those negatives into positives no matter what issue I'm facing. Of course, this is easier said than done, but you can start by simply changing your perspective and outlook about things that occur in your life. Remember, nothing changes if nothing changes—don't let that go over your head. Sometimes things aren't as personal as we think they are. We can move better in life when we use the assumption of positive intent instead of making a judgment about someone based off past experiences with others.

I am constantly faced with regret when I look back on how differently I could've handled some things that occurred in my life. I know everything happens for a reason, but that doesn't mean we can't be upset about it. We can easily see what we gain when we have self-control and confidence, and what we can lose when we don't. In every part of your life, you will be tested—you will pass some, you will fail some. Either way, you will learn something from it. What you learn and what you choose to do with it will help you become a better person, partner, parent, and friend.

CHAPTER 3:

LEARN FROM LOSSES

THE SAYING GOES "YOU LIVE, YOU LEARN." I HAVE a hard time believing that because most of us don't live. What I mean is that a lot of people play life on safe mode; they don't live to their fullest potential or productivity. They don't gamble on their dreams because they are afraid to lose, afraid the outcome might not be what they want it to be. For some, the risk is much greater than the reward. I can understand that in some circumstances. But to get something you've never gotten before, you've got to do something you've never done before. That's the law of success. If being successful was easy, then everyone would do it without a problem. The pursuit of our dreams means taking the road less traveled. That's the road of staying in your own lane, minding your own business, and executing the plan you have for *your* success.

I like to live by the saying "you *lose*, you learn," whether it be in sports, life, or relationships. Loss helps shape us to learn more. These losses can be painful, confusing, and often surprising, but they all have one goal, and that's to teach us a lesson. These losses can come at any time. Some of us endure them at an early age, and some of us don't encounter them until we're older.

One of my most prominent losses came the day I moved out of the house I lived in with my ex-wife and kids—the day I lost the ability to see my kids every day. It didn't register how much I would miss them till later down the road. Although I lost the ability to see them daily, I gained peace. Peace that I did the right thing by leaving, peace with myself for finally not being in a chaotic whirlwind of a relationship, and peace that my kids no longer had to endure the tension of an irreconcilable marriage. The peace came after the pain of suffering the loss. I went from taking them to school every day to seeing them every Tuesday and Thursday, plus every other weekend. I was somewhat satisfied with the visitation schedule, but it stung that I had a "parenting schedule" at all, especially since I am such an active father. During my marriage, I took my kids to all their extracurricular activities and was present for them in the ways they needed. I take pride in being a great father; it's one of the best things that's ever happened to me. And having that somewhat ripped away from me is something that I will have to deal with for the rest of my life. I still remember when my oldest daughter asked me, "Why can't you take us to school every day anymore?" It was a question that was so hard for me to answer because how do you properly answer that without letting the kids know about all the petty divorce litigation that occurs? As much as divorce hurts for the adults involved, it hurts ten times more for the kids who become innocent casualties in an oftentimes bitter war. I wanted and wished so badly that my ex-wife would just let go and be cordial for the kids. But when negative emotions are involved, things get hard to process.

I've learned many things from losing the ability to see my kids daily. One of them is to enjoy and engage more during my time with them. I started to realize that when our time with someone we love is limited, we start to cherish it more. We want to do things with them we've never done before. We learn to turn off our email notifications and put our phones down so we can be present in the moment. Hearing them laugh becomes sweeter, because we know we won't hear it the next day. It's a struggle a lot of men deal with when they're not romantically with their child's mother. Although the result may be a change in the time spent with your kids, I think it's okay to lose people, especially if they aren't good for you. It's best to have separate houses filled with peace, love, and structure than to be in one house filled with chaos, disrespect, and tension.

Divorce is ugly. It's full of loss, and it can change an individual for a lifetime. It can change how you show up in a relationship, and it can have a major impact on how you view the world relationally. Depending on what events affected you the most during your divorce, it can be directly tied to your vulnerability in relationships moving forward. It's up to you how it changes you. When it's all said and done, you can either be mad and bitter or healed and wiser. I chose to be on the better side of it all. I know that feelings are fleeting, so I knew there was no need for me to act out on them during my divorce litigation. Remember, reacting out of emotions can cost us a lot. Now, that doesn't mean I didn't have bouts of rage, sadness, and frustration, 'cause trust me, I sure as hell did. I would often cry and vent to friends to try and relieve some of the pain I was dealing with while also trying to understand how everything in my life went so left. The amount of emotional turmoil I was in is something I don't wish on anyone. I was constantly worried about the future, while also being haunted by my past. I found myself in this downward spiral of trying to figure out how to get past things I knew I had to go through in order to be a better man. The beauty of all of this is that I learned to be more emotionally intelligent by recognizing when I felt triggered by an event. I became more fiscally conservative after losing money, and worked harder after losing some bookings. I also learned what I want in a wife if I ever decide to marry again.

Lessons come from losses; what you learn from them is dependent on how much you value the loss. You can easily get yourself in a funk of self-pity over a loss, and it's hard to pull yourself out of that if you go in too deep. If you sit in shit too long, you'll forget what it smells like. So, you've got to understand that you aren't the first person to deal with this, and you won't be the last. What I'm going through is different from what you're going through, but we are all going through something. That's why it's so important to have compassion for other people even when you are down on yourself. Pulling yourself out of a dark place is difficult. I don't have all the answers; I just have advice from my own experiences to help educate others.

It's hard to see the light when you're in the dark, but eventually you've got to come out of there. You've got to start the process of dealing with your pain in order to get to peace. Try to worry less about how long it will take and focus more on the direction you are going; the end is what matters on your journey. For me, the pain I had to deal with centered around trust. I thought I would never be able to trust in a romantic partnership again after my marriage ended. Trust is a huge component in a relationship, and when you lose it because of distrustful actions, it can be hard to gain it back.

My marriage had ended emotionally before it did legally because of trust issues. When you can't rely on your partner to fulfill their duties in the relationship, you can easily lose trust and respect for them. But now I have realized that I can't hang on to what has happened in my past because it will ruin every relationship I try to have going forward. Bringing baggage to a destination that has everything you need is pointless. You are adding more clutter and stress to something that is peaceful and filled with joy. Losses can help you get rid of things that are holding you back from moving forward.

Perhaps you thought losing that job promotion was the end, but you didn't realize that losing that promotion caused you to apply for the job you've been scared to take on. In the process of doing so, you elevated to something greater. Something that adds more value to your life, something that helps you see more clearly and gives you purpose. Every loss you encounter isn't a terrible thing; some of those losses will turn into valuable lessons. Some of those losses are necessary for you to win in life. No matter what losses life hands you, there's always a lesson to be learned from them. What you learn can be used to not only better yourself, but you can use your life experiences to help others through counsel, simply walking with them through a similar circumstance. Let life's tests be your testimony. If you wake up the next day, know it's not over. Each day is a new beginning for you despite what has occurred the day prior.

Good Man: Education, Environment, and Empathy

Becoming a good man is about more than just being strong, brave, and responsible. It also involves using education to continuously better oneself, analyzing the environment to ensure prosperity, and using empathy to build meaningful connections.

Education is a powerful tool that can shape a person into a better version of themselves. It provides knowledge, skills, and critical-thinking abilities that can be applied to various aspects of life. As men, it is important to embrace education and use it to constantly improve ourselves. This could mean pursuing higher education, attending workshops and seminars, or simply reading and learning about new topics. Through education, we can develop a better understanding of the world and our place in it. We can also become more open-minded, compassionate, and empathetic.

A good man also constantly analyzes his environment. This means being aware of the people, places, and situations around us and understanding how they may impact us. By analyzing our environment, we can identify potential challenges and find ways to overcome them. We can also become more conscious of the effect our actions have on others and the world. This can help us make more informed decisions while also becoming more responsible individuals.

Empathy is another key aspect of becoming a good man. Empathy is the ability to understand and share the feelings of others. Being empathetic allows us to connect with people on a deeper level and build meaningful relationships. It also enables us to be more understanding and considerate toward others, which can lead to a more harmonious and compassionate society. Empathy involves actively listening to others, putting ourselves in their shoes, and showing genuine care and concern. It is a quality that can be developed through education and practice.

As men, we must recognize the importance of education, environment, and empathy in shaping us into good human beings. These three elements are closely intertwined and can greatly influence how we perceive ourselves, others, and the world around us. By incorporating them into our lives, we can become more well-rounded, compassionate, and responsible individuals. Being a good man is a continuous process. By constantly seeking knowledge, understanding our surroundings, and being empathetic toward others, we can become better versions of ourselves. Let's dive deeper into each of these elements, as we strive to be not just good men but also good human beings.

EDUCATION

As a society, we often strive to be better and more successful individuals. We try to be good people, to make a positive impact in society, and to leave a legacy that we can be proud of. But what exactly does it take to be a good man? Is it strength, intelligence, or a combination of both? While all these attributes are important, one tool that can greatly contribute to becoming a good man is education. Education is often seen as a means to obtain a well-paying job and financial stability. While this is certainly an important aspect of education, it is not the only benefit. Education also provides us with knowledge, skills, and critical-thinking abilities that can be applied to all aspects of our lives. Knowledge is power, and through education, we can expand our minds and gain a deeper understanding of the world around us.

When it comes to being a good man, knowledge is important, but wisdom is crucial. Knowledge is the ability to acquire information, but wisdom is the ability to apply knowledge to make a good decision. I am reminded of a quote from the late Miles Kington: "Knowledge is knowing that a tomato is a fruit; wisdom is not putting it in a fruit salad." Using these abilities allows us to make informed decisions and think critically about our actions and their impact on others. With education, we can learn about different cultures, perspectives, and ways of life. This not only broadens our understanding but also fosters empathy and compassion for others. In today's diverse society, these qualities are essential to being a good man. Being knowledgeable about the plights and adversities others face, whether it be due to race, gender, or religion, helps us understand how to better serve those in need.

Moreover, education equips us with practical skills that can be applied to our daily lives. For example, financial literacy is a crucial skill that is often overlooked in traditional education systems. However, being knowledgeable about financial management can help us make better financial decisions and achieve financial stability. This not only benefits us but also allows us to support and provide for our families and loved ones. Studies show that close to 70 percent of lottery winners go broke. Now, it's hard to imagine that happening to someone who has won hundreds of thousands or even millions of dollars. But the truth is, most people are not financially literate, which can lead them to misusing their earnings. This also tends to happen with professional athletes who suddenly find themselves rolling in money after signing million-dollar-plus contracts. It's important to know about taxes, investments, and passive income. Knowing these skills can help put you in a place to be more financially abundant in your life.

In addition to knowledge and skills, education also instills discipline and determination. Good men are not born; they are molded through hard work and perseverance. Education teaches us the value of hard work and encourages us to continuously challenge ourselves and strive for improvement. It also teaches us the importance of setting goals and working toward achieving them. These qualities are not only important in our personal lives but also in our careers and relationships. Lastly, education can empower us to work smarter, not harder. It opens doors to various opportunities and allows us to make connections and build relationships with like-minded individuals. With education, we can enter the workforce with a competitive advantage and have the skills and knowledge to succeed. This not only benefits us but also allows us to make a positive impact in our communities. Remember, using education as a tool to become a good man is a very wise decision. It equips us with valuable knowledge, skills, and qualities that can greatly contribute to our personal growth and success.

ENVIRONMENT

As human beings, we are constantly evolving and growing through our interactions with the world around us. Our environments play a major role in shaping who we are and the type of person we end up becoming. Being a good man is not just about having a kind heart or moral principles. It also involves being aware of our surroundings and adapting to them in a positive manner. Our environment has a significant impact on our thoughts, behaviors, and actions. Whether we realize it or not, we are constantly influenced by the people we interact with, the places we visit, and the situations we encounter. Therefore, it is essential to be mindful of our surroundings and understand how they affect us.

By analyzing our environment, we can identify the positive and negative aspects that impact our lives. For instance, if we surround ourselves with negative, toxic people, it can have a detrimental effect on our mental well-being. On the other hand, if we choose to surround ourselves with individuals who uplift and inspire us, it can have a positive impact on our character and outlook on life. Understanding the influence of our environment allows us to make conscious decisions and actively seek out spaces that align with our values and beliefs. Also, our environment provides us with endless opportunities for personal growth and self-improvement. It is like a playground full of challenges, obstacles, and events that can help us become stronger and better versions of ourselves. For example, being exposed to diverse cultures and different ideas can broaden our perspectives and help us become more compassionate toward others. Similarly, facing difficult situations can help us develop problem-solving skills, resilience, and mental stamina. Instead of seeing our environment as a hindrance, we should view it as an opportunity for growth and development.

On top of that, our environment reflects our inner state, which can serve as a mirror for self-reflection. If we find ourselves surrounded by chaos and disorder, it may indicate that we need to work on our own inner turmoil. In a similar sense, if we are constantly surrounded by negativity and conflict, it may be a sign that we need to address our own negative attitudes, behaviors, and possible traumas. Our environment can provide valuable insights into our own personal journey and help us identify areas where we need to improve.

Focusing on how we are products of our environment while also having the power to shape it in a way that aligns with our values and goals can help bridge the gap. So let's use our opportunities to create positive changes in our lives and the world we live in. As I sit here, reflecting on my own journey, I can't help but feel proud of how far I have come. I've faced challenges and struggles, but I've also experienced growth and success through it all. I have also learned the importance of surrounding myself with positivity and support. My environment has played a crucial role in shaping me into who I am today. The people I choose to surround myself with, the places I frequent, and the experiences I have encountered all have a significant impact on my mindset and behavior. I know it's not just about the external factors, but the internal ones as well. We also hold the power to shape our environment. We can choose to eliminate toxic relationships and negative influences, and instead, cultivate a space that encourages growth and development. Think about it: When we're constantly surrounded by negativity and doubt, it can be challenging to reach our full potential. But when we create an environment that supports our goals and values, it becomes a catalyst for our growth.

Let's be determined enough to use our environment to become better versions of ourselves. Let's surround ourselves with people who believe in us and push us to be our best. Let's seek out experiences that challenge us and help us learn and grow. Because it's not just about personal growth, it's about substantial growth. We also have the power to create positive changes in society and the community around us. By taking care of our environment and being mindful of our actions, we can contribute to a better and more sustainable future. We can choose to support causes that align with our values, enhance our societal footprint, and stand up for what we believe in. These small actions may seem insignificant, but they are exactly what it takes to make a long-lasting difference.

EMPATHY

Empathy is a powerful tool that we all have the ability to develop. It allows us to understand and share the feelings of others. In today's fast-paced world, empathy is often overlooked or undervalued. However, being a good man means utilizing empathy in all aspects of life. From our personal relationships to our interactions with strangers, empathy can greatly improve our lives and the lives of those around us. First, we have to acknowledge how empathy helps us build stronger and more meaningful relationships. When we take the time to understand and connect with others on an emotional level, we create a deeper bond. By empathizing with someone, we show them that we truly care about their thoughts and feelings. This can lead to stronger friendships, better romantic relationships, and a more supportive community. As the saying goes, "A friend in need is a friend indeed." By using empathy, we can ensure that we are there for our loved ones when they need us the most.

Not only does empathy strengthen our connections with others, but it also betters us as individuals. Empathy allows us to see situations from different perspectives and understand the complexities of human emotion, leading to personal growth and a better understanding of ourselves. By being empathetic, we become more open-minded and accepting of others' differences, helping us to improve our communication and conflict resolution skills, as we are able to see things from multiple viewpoints. In addition to personal relationships, empathy can also be used to make a positive impact in our community. It allows us to be more aware of the struggles that others may be facing and offer support and/or assistance when needed. Empathy can also drive us to take action toward creating a more inclusive, equitable, and understanding society. By putting ourselves in someone else's shoes, we can identify areas where change is needed and work toward that common goal.

Furthermore, empathy can be used in everyday situations to make a difference. It can be something as simple as offering a listening ear to a friend who is going through a tough time, or being patient and understanding with a customer service representative who may be having a bad day. These small acts of empathy can have a big impact and can make someone's day a little brighter. I personally remember how much the empathy others have had for me has gotten me through hard times. When I used to work as a food runner/server while also working as a full-time teacher, I was often tired, frustrated, and running on empty. Knowing this, others would help me during my shifts. For instance, if I was doing something for a table, a fellow server would refill the drinks of another table for me. It was these small acts that would make a difference for me and really warm my heart.

I must also say, it's important to note that empathy does not mean taking on the emotions of others and sacrificing our own well-being. It's about understanding and supporting, not fixing or solving. We should practice self-care and set boundaries to ensure we are not draining our own emotional resources while empathizing with others. You have to take care of yourself first so you can show up better for others. Fill your cup before you help fill someone else's.

Over the years, I have become more empathetic through my own personal life experiences. I have learned that empathy is a vital tool that we should use in our everyday lives. It not only helps us build stronger relationships to better ourselves, but it also allows us to make a positive impact in our community. By incorporating empathy into our daily interactions, we can create a more compassionate and understanding world. As individuals, we have the power to make a difference, and practicing empathy is a very crucial step in that direction, so let's choose empathy today, tomorrow, and every day thereafter.

CHAPTER 4:

YOU'RE THE PROBLEM

REALIZING YOU ARE THE REASON FOR WHY SOME of the things in your life have gone awry is a very strange yet liberating feeling. Holding yourself accountable for what happens in your own life is a game changer. But oftentimes nice guys like to play the blame game rather than looking at themselves and trying to figure out where they got it wrong. Exploring where your actions impacted your situation is vital to evolving as a man, and it's especially important for the evolution from nice guy to good man. The good news is that when you realize you're the problem, you also tend to find out that you're the solution as well. Knowing this allows you to think before you react, helps you with your self-control, and propels you to be less impulsive in your reactions.

Understanding what causes you to react a certain way can

help you navigate relationships, friendships, and environments and help you thrive in your journey. Being with people who hold you accountable will also make you better in life. It's imperative that we accept not only who we are but also who we are not. Being yourself is a small part of the ownership we take when we are evolving into someone better. Accepting the good parts and bad parts of who we are, along with taking accountability for our actions, is a recipe for growth in its purest form. Nice guys have the tendency to lack accountability and will often gaslight, manipulate, and deflect from their responsibility in the conflict that occurred. I call this being a coward, someone who runs away from their demons instead of facing them head-on.

Speaking of the word *coward*, I personally believe the word derives from the word *cow*. The reason I say that is because cows, in comparison to buffalo, are easily scared creatures. Buffalo and cows are very similar creatures, but one of the main things that stand out between them is how they react when they sense a storm coming. Cows often huddle together and run away from the storm. Doing this causes the cow to think that it's escaping the storm, but in reality the storm is still coming. The cows run until they are physically exhausted, causing them to move slower and slower, which eventually forces them to stop running. When this happens, the storm has caught up to them, and they are standing in the midst of the very thing they were running from. As they stand in the storm, out of breath, tired, and probably confused as to how this happened, they are forced to deal with what the storm brings. They have to absorb the rain, feel the thunder, and be frightened by the lightning. Meanwhile, buffalo huddle together to run toward the storm;

the buffalo knows it will encounter the storm and chooses to do so. They will use their might and courage to power through the storm, and by the time the buffalo is tired and out of breath, the storm has already passed. They stand in sunshine, thankful to have gotten through it.

I use this reference of buffalo versus cows as a comparison to good men versus nice guys. Nice guys are the cows (cowards)—they run from conflict and problems, often doing everything they can to get away from them. Good men are the buffalo running toward these issues in their lives, which minimizes the amount of pain, time, and frustration they experience from the storm. It's easy to be a cow when things get rough, when things don't seem like they are going your way, and life has you in a chokehold. But understanding that it will catch up with you regardless makes running away seem pointless. Because when you think about it in the long run, it is exactly that: pointless. Being a buffalo is a lot harder and more intimidating but allows you to confront what the problem is and find a solution more quickly.

A good man understands he can only control himself; he is not in control of others or what happens in his life. He knows he's only in control of his reactions. My outlook on life is that it consists of 10 percent of what happens to you and 90 percent of how you respond to it. Look at the definitive moments in your life and consider how this may be true. Choosing how to approach a problem is one of the most important things we can do in life. Problems always arise, and to keep them from going awry, we must rise to the occasion. Running away from them is not one of those ways. Another lesson from the buffalo/cow metaphor is knowing how they stick together. The cows run away from the storm with a group of other cows. The buffalo run toward the storm with a group of other buffalo. This is true in the human perspective as well; most nice guys hang out with other nice guys. They do this because they don't want to have their process of running away interrupted by someone who would rather run toward the storm.

This goes back to the old saying that our elders always told us growing up: "You are the company you keep." If you hang around losers long enough, you will become a loser. If you hang around people who are no good, then you, too, will eventually be no good. We draw from those around us, so if you're on this journey to becoming a good man, it's important to surround yourself with other good men. Men who will run into storms with you, men who will hold you accountable, raise you up, and ultimately push you to become a better man.

You may have these men in your life already, or it may take some time to find them. If you don't have them in your life, let me give you guidance on how to find other good men. One of the main character traits to take note of is their response to adversity. A man's response to an adverse situation says a lot about him and who he is. If he can stay calm, move with poise, and find his way out of it, then he's someone you need to surround yourself with. If he responds by lashing out or does anything other than finding a solution in a stoic manner, then you need to re-evaluate if you need him in your circle. Either way, finding the right circle is a part of your journey. The company you keep is going to play a major role in how your life turns out.

Shortly after starting the process of living alone, I began to understand and realize things about myself that brought attention to how and why some things didn't go the way I wanted them to. I realized that I was selfish, lacked accountability, and often ran away from issues in my life, especially in my marriage. Being selfish can be beneficial if done right, such as taking time to better yourself. Like I mentioned earlier, you can't fill others' cups if yours isn't filled first. In the past, I didn't do that. I used my "self" time to watch porn and chat with other women through DMs. I could've used that time like I use it now: to work out, journal, and focus on my journey of becoming a better man. I know now that I can't take back my actions. I can only learn from the things I did wrong, own them, and change within. I do believe that if I would have been open about it with my friends (my good men), they would've not only held me responsible, but they would have helped me get back on the right path. A good man will always be your accountability buddy when he sees you slipping. That's why iron sharpens iron (we will get more in depth about that later in the book).

It's a long, grueling process to have to look at the damage you caused in your own life. Growing and transforming into a good man is knowing that no matter what mistakes you made, you must focus on what you can do moving forward. For me, coming to the realization that I played a part in how my life turned out was eye-opening. Taking that step of accountability allowed me to put a plan into action, a plan that consisted of me making intentional moves and taking moments to help myself grow and heal. One of the most pivotal moves was changing how I interpreted my emotions, which is often called "emotional intelligence." After going to therapy and talking about all the demons I was dancing with, my therapist began to explain to me how anger is a secondary emotion. He began to give me various scenarios of how this comes into effect. He started with a driving experience: "Imagine you're driving with your kids in the car. You're cruising, listening to music, and enjoying your drive. Then suddenly, someone cuts you off, and you have to react with urgency by slamming on your brakes, honking at them, etcetera. You end up cursing, getting heated and angry because of what they did." I agreed with his sentiments and said yes, I would be pissed off. I would probably be doing all of that. He then asked why. I responded, "Because they were careless and cut me off. I could've gotten into a wreck and hurt myself or my kids." He then said to me, "Is it safe to say your primary emotion was fear? Fear that you would have wrecked, fear of your daughters being injured?" I said yes, for sure. It was then that I realized that my initial emotion was fear, but it was overpowered by anger.

Anger tends to overpower our real feelings. When plans change, we often get disappointed, and sometimes we react angrily toward the person causing the change. This causes the person to become defensive, and then before you know it, you're in this cycle of arguments that have no resolution. But it can all be handled differently if we react accordingly. Having emotional intelligence to know what you're really feeling and how to respond appropriately can save you from a life filled with regret. Many of our boys and men are in prison because of how they reacted to disrespect, disappointment, and fear. The more we are able to teach our younger generations about this, the more we can change the outcome of the future for them.

Working on accountability for your own actions will help you avoid making the same mistakes again. A smart man acknowledges his mistake, but a wise man also learns from it and uses that knowledge to not repeat the same mistake. We live in a world where "cancel culture" is very prevalent; people make a mistake and pay for it their entire lives. I don't believe that is the right way to go about anything in life. People are very selective with their outrage; they have confirmation bias, cognitive dissonance, and conscientious stupidity. They will shame and cancel someone for doing something, but if someone they are fond of does the same thing, they'll explain it away as "a simple mistake." We can't demonize people for mistakes, especially if it's a one-time thing. We have to be given the chance to learn from those mistakes and not repeat them.

Now, I'm all for people being properly punished for things they did wrong, but we unfortunately live in a society where the punishments often don't match the crime. Everyone wants to play a role and have an opinion, but the people who prosecute the hardest are often the guiltiest. What I mean by that is someone who does things similar or maybe even worse will fiercely condemn the same action done by another to simply distract from their own wrongdoings. These people are dangerous individuals, and you should stay away from them. That's why having the right people around you is so important to the evolution of you becoming a good man. I never said this process was going to be easy; it's very hard acknowledging your old habits and trying to break them. But like I said in the beginning of this chapter, when you realize you're the problem, you also realize you're the solution.

CHAPTER 5:

KNOW MEANS NO

One of the greatest things about becoming a good man is knowing not only who you are but knowing who you are not. Most of us get so caught up in who we think we are that we often try to fulfill every purpose or role. My dad used to tell me, "Son, you can do anything, but you can't do everything." It's true when you think about it—we try to do so much and will spread ourselves thin trying to please other people. This is referred to as people-pleasing and is a typical characteristic of a nice guy. He will often say yes to things that don't suit him and exhaust his own mental health, pleasing others while not doing anything to better himself. For instance, in my former nice guy days, I said yes to everything because I didn't want to come off as an asshole. When I used to be an art teacher, there were plenty of times when I was asked to make signs, decorate things, and so on. Every time a teacher, administrator, or colleague asked me to do something along those lines, I said yes—even though most times I wanted to say no because I personally had too much going on.

    I was the head football coach, helped with the drama club, was writing my first book, and was building my personal brand at the time. On top of all that, I needed to have time for my two daughters. I often drove myself into a mental decline by accepting duties that I should have rejected. People-pleasing can be so draining because you are always considerate of everyone else's feelings but your own. I want you to think about times in your life when you've helped other people or said yes to their requests, but you really wanted to say no. Did it leave you feeling like your tank was empty or drained? Were you aware that you only said yes to avoid them being upset? If so, you may be a people pleaser. This is why knowing what you like, who you are, and what you're capable of can help you make better and more sound decisions. You can avoid unnecessary drama and conflict by simply saying no. Understand that "no" is a complete sentence. You don't owe anyone an explanation as to why you don't want to go somewhere or do something that is requested of you. A person who knows this very well is rapper and record producer J. Cole. There was a reason why he decided not to go forward with his Kendrick Lamar diss track. He made it, released it, then quickly realized doing that was not him. He apologized for his actions, retracted his statements, and deleted the record from all platforms.

    What we can learn from this is that even though J. Cole initially said yes and began to engage in this rap battle because of pressure he felt from fans, he concluded on his own that this wasn't doing any good for his heart and soul. In the realm of hip-hop, he was being clowned for bowing out and not engaging in the beef, but in the real world, he was standing on business. He stood tall on his principles and morals, and I, for one, find that truly admirable. As men, we can easily get baited into doing things we don't want to do simply because we want to prove we are tough. Knowledge is power. When you know who you are, you have the power to be in control of what you do. I like to say the more you know the more you can say no.

Surrounding yourself with "yes" men is not good for your circle. You need people around you who are going to say no to you and also respect when you say no to them. Stay away from people who guilt you for saying no. It's so easy to say yes, but it's not that easy to say no, especially to someone you care about. For example, you can't give someone money every time they ask for it just because you care for them. Eventually, you won't have any money for yourself. You need to take care of yourself, then if you have something left over, you can help others. Apply this same method to your time, love, and grace: Give yourself as much as you need first. When you do that, you can be more mentally free to take on other things. There's a reason why when the plane oxygen masks deploy, you are instructed to put yours on first before attempting to help anyone else. When you help others first, you're in a frantic state of mind because you can't breathe and are consciously worried about hurrying to get yours done as well. This can cause you to improperly help them and cause more harm than help. Applying this to your life can help you see the importance of needing to say no to certain things and taking care of yourself before you entertain the idea of people-pleasing for the benefit of someone else.

Knowing your worth can take you a long way as well. Whether it be in business or your personal life, when you know your worth, it can help you develop the confidence to reject things that don't serve you and accept things that will set you up to prosper. In this industry, I have to know my worth, what my platform provides, and what my audience brings. Being a content creator on social media isn't for the weak. You often have to navigate how to be at the top of your game; it's very competitive. So, when brands reach out to me, I know I can't accept every partnership. When I first started, I did because I didn't know any better and I was trying to make a name for myself by working with big brands. But as time went on, I was able to understand that everything isn't for me. Most brands wanted to lowball me or ask for unreasonable deliverables. I became confident enough to reject offers and sometimes negotiate higher rates. The thing is, when certain brands reach out to me, I know it's because they want to reach a specific demographic. Whether that was my Black audience, my body-positive audience, or my male audience, they wanted to reach them through me. That comes with a price, which some of my other Black influencers call the "Black tax." It's an extra amount of money we tack onto rates to compensate for reaching that specific demographic.

If you are someone with a special gift or talent and people want to pay for it, know your worth. Make sure you say no to propositions that don't properly compensate you or serve you. Saying no to something that isn't for you can open a door for something better that's meant for you. Don't block your own blessing by saying yes to everything. Before I signed with a talent agency, I was approached by a huge denim brand. They offered me a few thousand dollars in exchange for some Instagram posts and usage rights to the images I took. When they sent the agreement over for me to sign, I found a little hiccup that alarmed me. It basically said something about owning the rights to "Notoriously Dapper" for present and future usage. This was a red flag that stood out to me, and I emailed them about it. Up until that point, our communication had been very seamless; they would email me back within an hour of my contacting them. For some reason, they didn't respond to the email I sent asking about this point in the agreement for a few days. I actually had to follow up on the response because it felt like they were ghosting me. Their reply was very short and a bit nasty, and it threw me off guard because up until that point, everything had gone so well. But because I was on the verge of turning down the deal unless I got clarification, they seemed bothered by me taking the initiative to question it. This is why I'm so thankful to have an agent that can do this for me. Ultimately, the communication about that clause in the agreement ended our potential partnership. What I learned from that situation is that saying no gave me the ability to say yes to another brand. Because if I had gone through with that partnership, the exclusivity they were demanding of me to use my likeness would have prevented me from working with other brands.

Many nos can turn into that opportunity where the yes is everything you need. The more you know what is for you, the more you can get what is for you. Use discipline to stay motivated to get what you want. This goes for relationships too, fellas. More men need to practice this thing called "dick discipline." Not every woman deserves sexual access to you. Don't get me wrong—it is nice and is an ego boost to have women wanting to have sex with you all the time. This is a sign that you are attractive and have qualities that many women want. But you can't say yes every time a woman makes sexual advances toward you. You have to say no and practice some self-control. This allows you not to be so focused on that one thing—sex—and to focus on using discipline. On the flip side, a lot of nice guys believe that if you take a woman out to dinner and treat her well, she owes you sexual access. Let me be clear: Nice guys typically do that because they are performing, or some would say peacocking, to get a prize. Good men are doing it for the purpose of getting to know her to potentially go out on a second date. If you have the intention of performing solely to get a prize from someone, you should just go to a random bar and find someone with that same mindset.

Using dick discipline and discernment is not easy. Trust me, it's a lot harder than it seems, but when you put this into action, you can start to filter out what's good for you and what's bad. Some people don't have pure intentions or your best interest at heart; some people have ulterior motives. You could say yes to that one-night stand and possibly have the rest of your life to pay for it. Or you could say no to it and have the opportunity to say yes to the right one. I'm not saying you shouldn't explore and have fun, especially if you have no commitments, but have some discipline and choose wisely during the process.

From career to life to personal relationships, I hope you know and understand the benefit of saying no to things that don't suit you. You don't have to be the nice guy who pleases everyone with a yes. Be the good man who pleases himself with a no. If you've had a long day at work but your boys want to go out, get wasted, and look for chicks, but you're not up for it, say no. If you get a dream job offer but it doesn't feel right to you, say no. If you are in a situation where someone you're seeing wants to do something that you're not down with, say no. More people respect a man who can say no to something and stand firm than someone who says yes to everything. People take advantage of you if they can see you will oblige to anything. This is why a lot of nice guys finish last (that's chapter 8). Keep your eyes open, head up, and chest out. You didn't come this far to digress. You came this far to move forward in progress.

CHAPTER 6:

GOOD MEN DO GOOD SHIT

WE ALL WANT TO DO GOOD IN THIS LIFE. Doing the good thing sometimes comes with people looking at you in a different light. Most people want to play it safe and do nice things. What does that mean? If you're ever in a situation where someone is doing something you know is wrong and don't approve of, the good thing is to take action, tell them to stop, and voice to them why it's wrong. The nice thing is to ignore what they are doing to save face or to avoid hurting their feelings. Understand, good men do not avoid conflict, in fact they face it willingly. There will be moments in life where you are called to be a good person and take action for the greater good. Sometimes there will be moments where doing the good thing can be perceived as not nice. Rapper and actor LL Cool J said it best: "If a little old lady is walking down the street and some guy grabs her pocketbook, then you grab the guy and break his nose and break his arm. You're not a nice guy but you're a good guy." That's what good men do. They don't stand around and let people who are defenseless get bullied, beaten, or attacked. Now, I'm not telling anyone to go out there and be Mr. Vigilante. Be smart enough to know the difference; you're not a superhero, you're a human. Life isn't a comic book series.

Good men often have to do things that aren't nice, but they mean well. If you're in the position at your job to hire and fire people, there may come a time when you have to fire someone. That's not necessarily a nice thing, but it's sometimes a good thing for the greater benefit of the company. Nice guys will avoid confronting you on your bad work performance, give you too much grace, and not hold you accountable. Then when it's time to fire you, you are caught off guard because you didn't see it coming. You felt as though your boss was okay with your performance and that your firing is unjustified. A good man will put you on notice, hold you accountable, and give you the chance to improve. But when you have failed to meet the standards he has provided for all his employees, then you have to go. A good man knows that one person can ruin the environment for everyone.

This happened a lot when I was an art teacher. In a class of over twenty-five kids, it only took one to disrupt and ruin the lesson for everyone else. We live in a world where this is too commonly accepted. In the grand scheme of things, it's truly unacceptable for one person to ruin something for others. I can remember a lesson I was teaching about the primary colors (red, blue, and yellow), and how they are combined to make secondary colors. I came up with a Roy Lichtenstein pop art–inspired assignment, where the students got to choose any cartoon character to draw. They then were instructed to draw the cartoon character and fill it in using only primary colors along with mimicking the iconic "dot" effect Lichtenstein often used in his work. Over the week, kids were working diligently and getting it done. I would assist them when they needed help, but for the most part they got the hang of it. Because my class was a related arts class, kids that had behavior issues in other classes would sometimes be moved to my class during that period.

One day, I got a new student who had behavior issues in music class, so they switched him to art. Like with all my students, I welcomed him with grace and love. I told him my rules and how I got down, and he seemed to be fine with what I expected of him. I then instructed him to start on the assignment we were working on. I talked to him separately about the primary colors and how they need to be used in the assignment. He said to me, "I'll use red and yellow, but I'm not using blue. My set [gang] I rep won't let me." You can only imagine the look on my face. I proceeded to tell this kid (who was in the sixth grade) that this is an educational environment, and I don't care what he does when he gets home, but while he's under my authority for fifty-five minutes, he has to do what I ask of him. He, of course, began to talk back to me and be disrespectful, and I am not the kind of teacher or adult that argues with children. I'm just not built like that. If you don't want to follow rules or the instructions I give you, then you have to suffer the consequences. Generally, I had a good rapport with all my students, whether they were gang-affiliated or not. Most of the kids loved me, and they respected me because I treated them all equally and demanded excellence out of them. That was not the case with this student.

This kid kept running his mouth after I told him to leave the classroom. He got louder and louder, trying to make a scene. My other students started to get upset with his antics, and another male student stood up and told him, "You're doing too much. Mr. Davis asked you to leave." They started going back and forth while I waited for an administrator to come to my classroom. The tension increased. I tried to de-escalate the conflict, but the new student got violent. He started throwing things in my classroom, screaming, and being completely out of control. During this scene, he hit one of my special-needs students with an object. The male student that was arguing with him then decided he was going to take care of it himself. Before I could even start to check on the student who got hit, they started going at it. As they were throwing punches left and right, the other students were getting up and running out of my classroom to get away. I was trying to break up the fight, and in the midst of this, I got hit with a few blows as well.

Finally, after everything was said and done, both kids were tired and still filled with rage, and the school resource officer finally arrived. They took both kids out of the classroom and instructed the other students to go back to class. It was so difficult for those kids to continue working for that last thirty minutes. They had just witnessed two young adult male students exchange heavy punches. Most of the students helped me pick up the supplies that were thrown around the classroom, asking me if I was okay, checking on me, and trying to reassure me that it wasn't my fault and that the newer kid had a lot of issues with other students and teachers. After class ended, I was called to the main office to give a statement about what happened. I told the principal what occurred, and I vouched for the kid who tried standing up for his classmates. After recounting the altercation in my head, I noticed that he didn't decide to get violent until the new student threw things and hit other innocent students in the process of his tantrum. I immediately put myself in his shoes, having been in a similar predicament before where I had to act violently in order to keep others safe.

I was a sophomore in high school and a student in my art class tried to stab another student with a pair of scissors. I threw a chair at him while he was charging the other student. At the time, it was just a reflex and something I felt compelled to act on. Because of this experience, I had empathy for my student who did the same thing. Although what he did wasn't nice, it was good. Even though chaos broke out, and I was struck with some blows in the crossfire, his intentions were to stop the kid from potentially harming other students. I typically don't condone violence of any kind, but I know sometimes it's necessary. I wasn't the only person who felt that way either.

While I didn't know the fate of both students, I was hoping the student who threw things was going to get a much heavier punishment than the other student, because in my mind, none of this would have happened if he had acted like he had some damn sense. Toward the end of the day, I had my second sixth-grade class, and of course word travels fast in a school, especially a middle school.

While the students were going to class, teachers were instructed to be in the halls during the exchange to help direct them to where they needed to be. I would often see some of my students from the first related arts class while waiting for my next class. As students were walking by me, they asked me if I was good and gave me high fives like they normally did. Then I saw my student from the first class (the one who defended the other students). I was low-key happy to see him because that meant he wasn't suspended or punished for what happened earlier in my classroom. He walked up to me and said, "Mr. Davis, I want to apologize to you for how I acted earlier and for fighting that kid." I was floored at his apology; I told him it was all good and that he did the right thing. We didn't have much time to elaborate on what happened, but we had a mutual understanding of his actions. I wanted to assure him that I wasn't upset or disappointed in him. I wanted him to know that I was proud of him. In my eyes, he did a good thing, although it wasn't nice, and he deserved to know that. He deserved to know he acted like a good man.

Even at a young age, you can make the choice to do a good thing. There are men twice his age who would never take the initiative to restore order. Good men like that need to be celebrated because those are the men who make people feel safe. Good men don't need to be praised for their actions. They act on purpose instead of performance, while nice guys do performative good deeds, putting on a show in hopes of people celebrating them. They thrive off that—just like the person who films themselves feeding the homeless and handing money to strangers. If you are doing it for the clout, clicks, and likes, the outcome of what you're doing seems inauthentic even though your intention may be good. Ask yourself, what's the purpose of doing this? The purpose should be for you to do the good deed or kind act because you want to do it and want to help someone, not so people will be pleased with you. You shouldn't care if there's a crowd, let alone a camera, around. You do it for the purpose of doing good, not for the performance of being nice.

BE A GOOD MAN, NOT A NICE GUY

The more people can truly dissect this and learn what it means to do good, the closer we'll get to living in a more authentic world where ulterior motives are less common, and these actions can be accepted with open arms.

It's unfortunate, but we have created a world where if someone does something good for you, you feel like you owe them something. Saying thank you should be good enough. Why do we need praise from strangers on social media or in society to be good men? We need to bring back a time when men did things without expecting verbal praise, recognition, or even sexual favors. Leave the good people alone, and stop ruining people's perception of receiving good deeds with your bad performative behavior and antics.

Many, including myself, can testify that all nice guys are nice till you don't give them what they want; then they turn into the victim (as in *no more Mr. Nice Guy*). I have been this guy, the guy who gives a compliment in hopes of getting a phone number, the guy who does something nice for the praise it will garner. When I didn't get what I expected, I would play the "nice guys always finish last" card. But it's true; nice guys do finish last. They finish last because most people can see right through them. Stop expecting praise for being a nice person. Instead, do good things with a purpose, and be a good man, because good men do good shit.

Three Currencies of Life: Time, Money, and Health

As we go through life, we are constantly juggling work, relationships, and personal endeavors along with managing our time, money, and health. These three currencies of life—time, money, and health—hold immense value and play key roles in shaping us into better individuals.

TIME

Time is something that is limited for all of us. No matter how rich or poor we are, time is one of the only equalizers.

BE A GOOD MAN, NOT A NICE GUY

When our time runs out, it's gone, and we can never buy time back no matter how much money we have. However, it is what we do with the time we have that sets us apart from one another. Therefore, managing our time is of utmost importance. As the saying goes, "time is money." We should use our time wisely and invest it in things that matter to us. This not only helps us achieve our goals but also gives us a sense of satisfaction and fulfillment. Nice guys have poor time management skills and will poorly utilize their time, using it to satisfy their vices rather than improve themselves. A good man will see time as a way to make it work for him. Nice guys count time; good men make time count. What I do with my time now as a good man compared to what I did with it as a nice guy is truly a night-and-day difference. Idle time, if not used correctly, can negatively affect the production of your day. I now like to use my time to dedicate myself to things that enhance me as a man.

I started working out more and set goals on the bike rides I would do. I started by setting a goal of five miles; eventually I got to twenty miles. Using my time to hit tangible targets gave me a sense of pride. It also helped me maintain discipline in my life. If I said to myself that I was going to get up at seven in the morning to ride my bike for ten miles, then I was going to do it. The important thing is to keep the promises you make to yourself.

When I was a nice guy, I used my time to fulfill vices that had nothing to do with me becoming a better man. Playing video games all day, eating unhealthily, not being active, and watching porn—that is a recipe for disaster.

Even typing it out right now makes me cringe. How was I ever going to become the man I am today if I was still using my time in that manner? The answer is, I wouldn't have become him, and I wouldn't be giving you advice right now. I would be stuck until I hit rock bottom, and let me tell you something: When you hit, you hit hard. Consider this an ultimatum: Change now for the better or continue down the path of destruction.

We know time is something we all have, and it is something we can never get back once lost. The seconds, minutes, and hours tick away without any pause or rewind button. This is why it is crucial to understand the importance of time and to use it effectively. Being a good man also means being punctual and respecting other people's time. It shows our commitment and responsibility toward our work, relationships, and events we attend. Nice guys tend to have difficulty with punctuality and respecting others' time. They often give off entitled main character energy when they finally do deign to show up somewhere. There's a common saying: "We all have the same twenty-four hours in a day." It's true, and it is up to us to make the most out of it. We can do this by prioritizing our tasks and avoiding procrastination; we can utilize our time effectively and achieve success in all aspects of our life.

When we think of things that cripple us mentally, it's usually during a state where we aren't being productive. When we are productive, our mind is focused on the task, and no matter how stressful the task is, our mind is helping us power through it to achieve the goal. When we are alone and not being productive, intrusive thoughts come into our head, driving us to worry about things that haven't even happened or possibly will never happen.

Good time management is a major factor in achieving success. Most good men have great time management skills. Perhaps you've heard the phrase, "timing is everything." This holds true in many aspects of life. Whether it is in our career opportunities, relationships, or personal growth, timing plays an important role in determining our success. By using our time effectively and seizing opportunities when they present themselves, we increase our chances of achieving our goals and reaching our full potential. That's why you have to stay ready, so you don't have to *get* ready. But also, don't get discouraged by things not happening when you think they are supposed to. Yes, time is everything, but more importantly, God's timing is everything. Have patience with your time and what you do with it. Some things take longer than others. Good men are patient and trust the process.

Our time is a precious and limited resource that should not be taken for granted. It's never too late to start living the life you want. Start by setting goals for yourself, big or small, and work toward them every day. Whether it's learning a new skill, traveling to a new place, or simply taking time to do something you enjoy, make sure you are actively living in the present moment. I can't stress enough the importance of using our time wisely as good men by prioritizing tasks, investing in ourselves, and seizing opportunities when they arise. By doing so, we can achieve success and fulfill our goals, while living a more meaningful and fulfilling life. So, the next time you find yourself thinking that you have all the time in the world, remember that time is slipping away with every passing second. Be a good man and use your time wisely. As you continue with the time you're given, make a conscious effort to create a purpose out of your time. We often get caught up in the busyness of life and forget to truly live in the moment.

MONEY

Another life currency is money, which some consider the most valuable currency in today's world. It is crucial to manage our finances wisely to ensure a secure future for ourselves and our loved ones. Just as we budget our time, we must also budget our money. This means being mindful of our expenses and saving for emergency situations. Money management also involves having financial goals and working toward them consistently. Whether it is planning for retirement, paying off debt, or investing for long-term stability, responsible money management can help us achieve financial independence and security. Moreover, being financially responsible also reflects our character and values as individuals.

Money can often be presented as the backbone of our modern society. This is a topic that is regularly discussed and debated politically, religiously, and even personally. It is sometimes seen as a metric of success and fulfillment.

This thinking can create a skewed view of what success means to us as a society. Money can also have the power to corrupt and cause harm. However, money itself is neutral—it is the way we use it that ultimately determines the level of impact it has. After all, money is the most replenishable asset we have on earth. Unlike time, we can always find a way to get our money back if we lose it.

Let's further understand the importance of money and how we can use it for good. First and foremost, money is necessary for our survival and well-being. It provides us with the means to access basic necessities such as food, shelter, and health care. Without money, we would not be able to support ourselves and our loved ones. It also allows us to have a better quality of life by providing us with opportunities for education and personal growth. In essence, money is an essential tool for our survival and progress.

When money is used for selfish or unethical purposes, it can have detrimental effects on individuals and society. The pursuit of wealth at any cost has led to various issues such as income inequality and exploitation of resources. The love of money has also been linked to greed and corruption, causing harm to innocent lives. This highlights the importance of using money responsibly and ethically. As a good man, it's important to use your money in a reasonable and ethical way. For example, gambling your money away is not smart. Nice guys have bad money habits; they buy things they don't need and spend money on things like sex, gambling, alcohol, and drugs. I don't judge anyone for their vices and what they do, but I can tell you firsthand that quitting drinking has been a cheat code for me. Not only do I save money, but I physically feel a lot better. The thing is, I already have a bubbly and outgoing personality, so I didn't need to be drunk to become a social being. I have known many men who have not only ruined themselves but also ruined their families because of mismanaging their money. As a man, you need to be trusted when it comes to spending money. Your spouse needs to know you can still pay the bills and provide food for the family. Gambling addiction is a real thing; people feel a high from the adrenaline. Losing your money to addictive habits will always cost you a heavy fine. If this is something you struggle with, then you need to seek professional help. It's okay to get help for things by seeking refuge. Doing this can encourage you to find the discipline to fix any issues that may be holding you back from reaching your full potential. Don't wait till you lose all your money fulfilling vices and bad habits you've adopted over time to realize you need help.

As a good man, it's also imperative to use money as a force for good in our society. Through charitable donations and philanthropy, individuals and organizations can use their wealth to make a positive difference in the world. From supporting education and healthcare initiatives to funding research for important causes, money can be used to bring about meaningful change. Similarly, some government programs can utilize your funds for social welfare programs and infrastructure development, benefiting the entire community. This is why the more money we make, the more taxes we are expected to pay. Money also has the power to create jobs and boost economic growth. When individuals or businesses invest their money in ventures, it leads to more opportunities for employment and contributes to the overall development of the economy. This results in a cycle of prosperity where the more money circulates, the more it can benefit individuals and our society as a whole.

Money is a very powerful tool that can have both positive and negative impacts on our lives and society. It is important to recognize its value and use it wisely for the greater good. Whether it is through charitable acts, investments in worthy causes, or responsible spending, we have the ability to use money for good. Let us strive to create a world where money is used to uplift and support each other rather than tear us apart.

HEALTH

Finally, to live a happy and fulfilling life, we must take care of our physical and mental well-being. Our bodies and health are our most precious possessions, and we must prioritize a healthy lifestyle above everything else. We should maintain a healthy diet, exercise regularly, and take care of our mental health by engaging in activities that bring us joy and peace. Being a good man also means taking care of the health of those around us, including our family and friends. We can do this by encouraging our friends and family to get health checkups and be there for them in times when they are ill. We should encourage and support others in maintaining a healthy lifestyle. By managing our health, we can improve the quality of our life and be more productive in achieving our goals.

We all know that being healthy is important, but how many of us can say we prioritize it in our own lives? Whether you're currently a good man or nice guy, in today's fast-paced world, it's easy to get caught up in the day-to-day hustle and bustle and neglect our health. We do this by always being on the go and then grabbing fast food because it's the easiest thing to get in the moment. We constantly fill our time chasing the American dream and we can forget to stop, breathe, exercise, and seek refuge for ourselves. However, the truth is that being healthy is a major factor for not just our physical well-being but for our mental and emotional well-being as well. Being a good man means seeking help when you don't feel well. This goes for physical and emotional pain. It's okay to seek therapy if you're struggling with something internally. Most of us try to be all macho and suffer through the pain. There is no need for that in this time of modern medicine and health care. We can get help to heal just about any sickness nowadays.

One of the most obvious reasons why being healthy is so important is that it helps to reduce the risk of developing illnesses and diseases. By maintaining a healthy lifestyle, we can prevent some health issues such as heart disease, diabetes, and obesity. As I mentioned previously, during my nice guy days, I had developed bad habits. One of them was eating very unhealthily, and I wasn't active either. Because of this I was diagnosed with type 2 diabetes in 2021. Now I am *forced* to put my health first. If I would have done that in the first place, I wouldn't be dealing with the high risk of heart disease and stroke. Putting our health first not only saves us from physical pain and discomfort but also saves us from the high medical expenses that come with these conditions. In fact, according to the World Health Organization, more than two-thirds of all deaths worldwide are caused by non-communicable diseases, most of which are preventable by maintaining a healthy lifestyle.

As a good man, understand that being healthy also has a significant impact on our mental well-being. Studies have shown that regular exercise and a balanced diet can help alleviate stress, anxiety, and depression. Nice guys, take notes here: When we take care of our bodies, we feel more energized, confident, and capable of handling life's challenges. On the other hand, an unhealthy lifestyle can lead to low self-esteem, negative body image, and even mental health disorders.

Another important aspect of taking care of your health is the impact it has on our productivity and quality of life. When we are in good health, we have more energy and stamina to carry out our daily tasks. We can focus and have a clearer mind to make better decisions. This translates into better performance at work or school, leading to a more fulfilling life. When we lead an unhealthy lifestyle, it can make us lethargic, unmotivated, and prone to frequent illnesses, which can hinder our ability to achieve our goals and live our life to its fullest potential.

Apart from the physical and mental benefits, being healthy can also have a positive impact on our relationships, especially our sex lives. There is nothing worse than getting intimate and not being able to fulfill the duty because you're out of shape. Good men have good sex, and it's important to be able to please your partner. When we are in good health, we can be more present and engaged in our relationships. We can participate in activities with our loved ones and create happy memories together. On the contrary, a poor state of health can limit our ability to enjoy quality time with family and friends, causing strain in our relationships and ourselves.

Time, money, and health are the three currencies of life that we should value and manage with extreme wisdom. They are interconnected, and finding a balance among them is essential for a prosperous, wholesome life. Being a good man involves being responsible for managing these three aspects effectively. By doing so, we can lead a fulfilling life and inspire others to follow our lead. So let us make the most of our time, money, and health and strive toward becoming the best version of ourselves. We have the power to shape our own future and create a legacy of being a good man who will be remembered for generations to come.

Good Man: Providing, Protecting, and Patience

Providing, protecting, and showing patience are three key elements that will contribute to creating a safe environment for you and those around you. Whether it is at home, in the workplace, or in society as a whole, these three principles will be essential for you to maintain a sense of inner security while also promoting the safety and well-being for those you're responsible for. As we all know, we are currently living in a world filled with all sorts of challenges and uncertainties. This ranges from global tensions to political turmoil, from environmental issues to economic struggles. We are continuously faced with matters that require us to be on our toes, be present, and be aware. In order for you to provide, protect, and have patience, you must be experienced in life.

I read somewhere that most men will receive flowers only on their graves. When I thought about the societal evidence to back this up, it's true. Most men will never receive flowers when they are alive and well. Life has shown me in many ways that as a man, there is little to no benefit or gain in being innocent; most men have to trade their innocence early in life and sometimes at a young age in exchange for experience, whether that be fighting on the playground, getting in trouble at school, or even getting involved in things we shouldn't be doing. We have been taught that there's no value in lacking experience as a man; experience comes with being battle-tested. What I mean by this is that most men are able to be functional members of society due to their life experiences. Personally, my experiences as a young Black boy prepared me for how the world works. I can read rooms, improvise, and, as some would say, I know how to move in a room full of vultures.

PROVIDING

Providing plays a crucial part in creating a safe environment. It stems from the provision of basic needs such as food, shelter, stability, and education. When you are able to provide these necessities, the people around you are more likely to live a secure and healthy life. I know from my experience in the education system how important this is. Students who come from environments without a provider sometimes act out during class. It's hard to focus on getting your lesson done if your mind is racing about what uncertainty you have to deal with when the school day is over. For some kids, the only food they got were school-provided meals. I would see a huge difference in how certain students acted after they had lunch. It's hard to concentrate on long division, let alone an art teacher telling you the history of the color blue, when you are too concerned about being hungry because you didn't have any dinner last night. Having the provision of stability is something we take for granted every day—that is, until we meet someone or encounter a situation that humbles us to count our blessings.

Being a provider is more than just a title or role; it is a responsibility that comes with great duty and significance. One could argue that's why many men abandon the role of fatherhood; they get too overwhelmed with the thoughts of having to take on that high level of responsibility. Providers are people usually responsible for the care and provision of someone or something, and we can all agree that it is a lot easier to take care of some*thing* than some*one*. The accountability required for showing up for another human is far greater than showing up for something. Providers play a huge role in ensuring the well-being and growth of those under their care or supervision. It could be a family member, a community, or an organization. People who depend on you need you to show up for them.

I was faced with this dilemma when my ex-wife first got pregnant. We were still kids in college, with reckless habits. We had a casual relationship at the time, nothing serious at all—just two kids drinking, partying, and hooking up. When she got pregnant, it felt like time stood still. I was twenty-two years old at the time and was so unsure about my life, as was she. We had a lot of decisions to make, and we were in no position to be parents. When she got pregnant, all eyes were on her because everyone wanted to know if she was going to keep it or have an abortion. As we weighed our possibilities and chose to move forward with the pregnancy, I was put on this pedestal with all eyes on me. People wondered if I was going to stay with her and build a family, break up with her and co-parent our child, or abandon her and the child completely. I knew I wanted to do the right thing, or at least try to. So, I stayed with her and attempted to make this wild, unforeseen situation work out for the best. During the process of figuring it all out, it dawned on me why so many men abandon the situation altogether. You quickly realize how much of a responsibility it's going to be, and if you don't have much life experience caring for a child, or even lack responsibility, you will run from challenges instead of facing them. I was fortunate enough to have the solid foundation of my parents, especially my father, who taught me how to prosper in the face of adversity.

He taught me that one of the main aspects of being a provider is not only providing the basic necessities but also meeting the needs of those you're responsible for. This can include physical, emotional, spiritual, and financial needs. For example, my father is a great provider. I never had to worry about not having anything I needed. I'm not just talking monetarily. I didn't grow up a rich or wealthy kid, but he ensured we had food, shelter, and most importantly love. I have never felt unloved by him, and I knew he was the most unselfish man on earth. He would do everything for my sister and me, he understood the needs of those under his care, and he always did his best to fulfill those needs daily. Similarly, if you're a business owner or boss, you take on the role of being a provider for your employees and staff. You must ensure they have a safe, stable, and productive work environment. Not being able to provide this can cause people to lose trust in you, and they will be less motivated to work harder for you.

In addition to meeting these needs, providers must also have a sense of compassion and grace. Having the ability to provide with compassion is next level; when you're able to do that, those around you will be less likely to take it for granted. They will recognize that you are doing this for the benefit of them and not yourself. Most nice guys will provide, but they will provide with conditions attached. They will fulfill your needs but only if you praise them, say thank you constantly, or give them something in return. On the contrary, a good man will do it because it's his duty as a provider. He doesn't need the praise (although it's nice) because that's not what motivates him to provide for others.

Providing with grace can be challenging sometimes because you want to hold people accountable for making mistakes to ensure things go smoothly and that they are following the standard you have set. But we have to understand that grace is given to us every day, and we must extend that same level of grace when we are providing for others. We must allow space for some mistakes to occur and correct them as they happen. Being able to properly provide instructions and set expectations will allow more room for grace in your relationships, friendships, and partnerships. None of us are perfect, and sometimes we will get it wrong more times than we get it right, but that doesn't mean we don't deserve redemption; we all deserve grace and patience.

Along with patience, compassion is something I have struggled with my entire life; I have always been the type to just keep it moving in difficult times. So sometimes, unless something traumatic happens, like a death, I have found it's hard for me to have compassion with people, especially when it comes to their own issues. But experience has helped me become more compassionate the older I get. I am able to step back and examine feelings and compare them to other emotions I've encountered in life. That's the beauty of being human: We get to have these good and bad experiences that help shape and sometimes redefine who we are as a person. From losing loved ones to gaining new insights and perspectives, the journey is filled with surprises that will humble you. Use your experiences from life to help guide you down the right path. We are all built to provide, you just have to provide with the right motives and circumstances. Be the good provider for those who are depending on you; just make sure you do it with compassion, grace, and empathy.

PROTECTING

Let's talk about the second element—protecting—which is all about ensuring the safety of individuals, whether it be physical, emotional, or psychological. Doing this includes creating and enforcing boundaries, establishing policies and procedures, and implementing safety measures. Protecting is a concept that is deeply ingrained in our human nature. From the time we are born, we are constantly surrounded by those who strive to protect us, including our parents, our caretakers, and our teachers. As we grow older, we start to learn in different environments. We learn in the classroom, on the playground, and on the streets. We begin to protect ourselves and those around us. There's a reason why when you are a kid you stand up for yourself when another kid is trying to take a block from you or is being mean to you. It's in your nature to protect yourself. Whether it is crossing the street safely or standing up for what's right, protection is a fundamental aspect of living and existing in a functioning society.

We live in a time where protecting has taken on an entirely new meaning, from the need to "protect your peace" to protecting against risks associated with the rise of technology and the internet. We must be aware enough to protect ourselves online from cyber threats, hacks, scams, and identity theft. Although we live in a more advanced society where we have self-driving cars and robots taking jobs from humans, the notion of protection can be traced back to the early days of civilization. Our ancestors learned to build shelters to protect themselves from weather and predators. They also developed weapons to defend themselves if attacked by other humans or animals. Those ancient instincts still live inside us today. We are vigilant and proactive in recognizing potential threats and taking the necessary actions to prevent any harm.

As a man, father, and friend, there is a certain type of responsibility that comes with these roles. Among the many things I strive to be, a protector is at the top of my list. This is a duty that all men must uphold with severe attention and the utmost dedication. To be a good man, you must provide a safe space for others. I can't reiterate this enough; this is one of the most desirable traits a man can possess. In society, we have labeled being a "man" as being tough and strong. While you need to be tough and have strength in certain circumstances, those are not the only things it takes to be a man. I believe that being a man, especially a good man, is not just about physical strength, but it is about standing up for what is right and defending those who need help. This could mean stepping in when someone is being mistreated or simply being there to offer support and guidance during difficult times. In today's world, dangers can lurk around every corner, so, naturally, being a protector is more important than ever. In the face of adversity, it is our obligation to stand tall and be a shield for those who cannot protect themselves.

My duty as a protector is amplified when it comes to my role as a father. Being a dad means taking care of my children, making sure they have everything they need, and ensuring they have a safe and nurturing environment to prosper in. Being a good father and man is about being their first line of defense against any harm that may come their way. This is why it was so important for me to start bringing my girls to church with me when I started to get more involved with the Word of God. The Bible is a strict, outlined book of stories, principles, and actions we need to help protect ourselves from evil. Just as we teach our kids to look both ways before crossing the street or how to defend themselves against bullies, it is our requirement as fathers to teach them faith and the guidance of God to provide them protection when we are not around.

My protective nature doesn't just stop with my own children and family. As a friend, it's my duty to look out for those I care about. Being a protector for my friends means being a listening ear, offering advice, and being there for them through thick and thin. I take it upon myself to help my friends in any way they need me. I will help them move heavy furniture, be the designated driver on a night out, babysit, and even provide them with some financial help if they need it. But I only do this if it doesn't cost me my peace. Like I mentioned earlier, it's okay to say no. Be there for your people whenever you can but don't do it at the expense of your own mental health. For instance, if you are barely getting by financially and your friend or family member asks you for money, it's okay to say no. Know your limits. You don't want to put yourself in jeopardy by overextending help you can't really provide. That's a nice guy move, and we are trying to be good men.

Speaking of finances, I'm reminded of a funny dad joke I used to say to my kids when they would ask for expensive things. I would say, "I'm so broke, I can't even pay attention." To me, that's another aspect of protection that's underrated: keeping my loved ones safe from bad moods by delivering a joke once in a while. It takes a special kind of skill to be able to produce a cheesy pun or a cringe-worthy one-liner that can make everyone laugh. That's where I come in and save the day with some comic relief. I'm always prepared with a terrible joke to lighten the mood and protect my children, family, and friends from bad moods and boredom.

Of course, there have been times when my protective instincts have gotten a bit out of control. I dread the day I have to meet my daughters' first boyfriends. My cousin Jamal and I have already rehearsed how it's going to go, like the scene from the movie *Bad Boys*, when a kid comes to pick up his daughter and they pretend to be jerks harassing the young man. Let's just say we might scare him off with some of our antics, but they will all be lighthearted fun. In all seriousness, he better be a good man and not a nice guy. I will have to vet them and make sure they have the right intentions with my daughters—that's my duty. I'm just keeping it real.

Being a protector comes with challenges, but I believe it's a responsibility that pays dividends in the end. And while it can be a bit tiring and maybe a bit overwhelming, there's nothing more rewarding than knowing you have the ability and knowledge to protect those you love dearly. It gives us a sense of purpose and satisfaction knowing that we are making a positive difference in the lives of the people we care about and those around us. I hope that my actions and words as a protector will inspire others to do the same. In the end, your role as a man, father, and friend will teach you the importance of being a protector. It's not just a duty; it is also a privilege to be able to safeguard those we care about. As I continue to fulfill this role with all my heart and purest intentions, I know that by protecting others, I am also protecting myself and creating a better world while setting the standard for future generations of men. To all my fellow protectors out there, keep doing what you do best. Keep those dad jokes and protective instincts strong. After all, it's what makes us the men, fathers, and friends we need to be.

PATIENCE

They say patience is a virtue, and as a good man, I have most definitely learned the value of it. Not just with others, but most importantly with myself. Let's face it, being a good man is not easy at all. There's always some sort of pressure on us to be strong, confident, and to always have the answers to a problem. When we think about what makes a good man, many traits come to mind, such as honesty, integrity, kindness, and courage. All these characteristics contribute to being a good man, but one of the most overlooked traits is patience. Patience is a crucial aspect of being able to control your temperament, emotions, and reactions. As men, we are often taught to be super strong and show little to no vulnerability. Some of us are encouraged to suppress our emotions and not let them get the best of us, but doing this can lead to impatience, which can turn into outbursts of anger or frustration. Having patience allows us to have grace with our emotions, to take the time to step back and think before we respond. It shows true strength and maturity to be able to stay calm and conduct yourself properly in difficult situations.

Patience also allows us to be more understanding and empathetic toward others. As men, we tend to focus on fixing problems rather than listening and understanding. This is a habit I'm guilty of all the time. However, I have learned to ask, "Do you want a solution? Or do you want me to just listen?" Doing this allows me to be more aware of what the person is asking of me with the conversation. I have noticed this has helped me build stronger relationships and shows that I care about what the person is saying and I respect their desired outcome of the conversation.

Furthermore, patience is an essential trait in achieving our passions, goals, and dreams. Most people have big ambitions and want to achieve them quickly—I call this the microwave syndrome. It's where we want instant glorification and gratification with as little effort as possible. But just like food cooked in an oven often tastes better than something cooked in a microwave, we all know true success takes time, effort, work, and patience. You must be willing to put in the hard work and wait for the results. When you are impatient, it can lead to you giving up quickly or making a rash decision that can hinder the future of your success. In this fast-paced world where instant success seems to be the norm, being patient has become a rare and more valuable trait to possess.

In relationships, patience is vital in building a strong connection with our partner. We can't expect things to happen instantly or for our partner to change overnight. Patience allows us to work through challenges while also communicating effectively, leading to a healthier and happier relationship. Being patient also means being able to handle difficult situations with grace and composure. As men, we will be faced with unexpected challenges, and it is how we handle them that defines us. Whether it be waiting for a job promotion, waiting for the right partner, or something as simple as waiting in line at the DMV, by being patient, we can learn to approach these situations calmly and find solutions rather than giving in to our frustrations. One of the most frustrating things to experience is waiting on something you have no control over. Like when you order food at a restaurant, and it ends up getting busy, and now the kitchen gets backed up with orders, and you have to wait. But I have found that if I focus on something other than the food, it makes the time go by faster, and I am in control of how I respond internally. Patience can really make or break us in moments like these.

Patience comes with accepting who you are, flaws and all. I mean, I'm not the most perfect man out there, in fact, I'm very far from it. I have my fair share of imperfections and mistakes I've made throughout life. But instead of beating myself up over them, I've learned to be patient with my own growth, improvement, and journey. And let me tell you, the process is not easy. It's like trying to grow a garden in the middle of a desert; it takes time, effort, and lots of patience.

Being patient with yourself means understanding that change doesn't happen overnight. You can't just wake up one day and expect to be a completely different person. It's a constant process of learning and unlearning, of making mistakes and trying again. And let's be real here, that takes a whole lot of patience. But an important aspect of a good man's journey is having patience with others, especially when they come from different backgrounds than us and may do things differently than we do. It's impossible for everyone to see eye to eye all the time. It's about having patience and understanding while also respecting others' perspectives, even if they're different from our own. When you encounter someone who is different from you in these ways, use it as a chance to learn from them. Instead of being judgmental, be curious about their experiences. You will find that although you are different in many ways, you may share some similarities. Always be open-minded and mindful of other people's perspectives and have patience for the way they do things.

Believe me, there are times when people will test your patience. Like when you're stuck in traffic, and someone decides to cut you off for no reason. Or when you're waiting in line at the grocery store and the person in front of you is taking their sweet time counting their coins or coupons. But as a good man, you learn to take a deep breath and remind yourself to be patient. Because at the end of the day, getting angry or frustrated won't make the person move any faster. So, if you want to be a good man, learn to be patient. Have patience in accepting who you are, patience in your own growth, and patience with others. We all know it won't be a cakewalk, but you know what they say: "Good things come to those who wait." Now, don't get me wrong; I'm not saying you should just sit back, relax, and wait for things to magically fall into place. In fact, patience also goes hand in hand with hard work and determination.

In this life, we must be patient with our progress. Success does not happen overnight. We must be willing to put in the time and effort to achieve our goals, even when it may seem like we are making slow progress. As fathers, we must be patient with our children. They may push boundaries and test our patience, but it is our role to guide them with love and understanding. Our patience will not only teach them important life lessons, but it will also show them how to handle difficult situations with grace. As friends, we must be patient with each other. We may have different paths in life and make different choices, but true friendship transcends all of that. We must be patient with each other's flaws and mistakes while continuing to support and encourage each other.

Patience is not just about the act of waiting; it's about how we wait. We can use these moments as time to reflect, learn, and grow. Next time you find yourself losing your cool or getting impatient, remember the wise words of our elders: patience is a virtue. And as a good man, it's up to you to embody it in all aspects of your life. Take a deep breath, count to ten, and approach the situation with a calm, collected mindset. Because in the end, your patience will not only benefit the people around you, but it will also bring you inner peace and happiness.

It may seem like a simple virtue, but patience has the ability to transform our lives and the lives of those around us. Find that balance of knowing when to push forward and when to take a step back and be patient. If you feel that you're in the right mindset to continue, then you can push forward, but if for some reason you feel as though you are struggling to continue, then take a step back. Taking a step back to analyze the situation can make all the difference in how things pan out. For example, if you are in a heated argument with someone you care about, it's important to step back, analyze, and then return later when emotions are not as high. Doing this gives you and the other party a way of coming to a more rational state of mind so you can find a resolution for the issue. Remember that true strength is not measured by how fast we achieve a resolution or a goal; it is measured by the patience and resilience we show along the way.

CHAPTER 7:

IRON SHARPENS IRON

Y**OU MAY HAVE HEARD THE SAYING "IRON SHARP**ens iron." This is a phrase from the Bible, Proverbs 27:17 (NIV): "As iron sharpens iron, so one person sharpens another," referencing how we as people can improve each other through collaboration, feedback, and challenges. But what does it mean to be iron? Being iron means you're tough, genuine, resilient, and determined. How can we as men apply this to our lives? And the bigger question is, are you iron? 'Cause if you're not, then iron won't sharpen you, it will destroy you. It will leave you in a state of dismantlement, confusion, and brokenness. But if you are iron, then you're strong, and when you choose someone else who shares your strength, you can expect their strength to sharpen yours as well. When you rub two iron blades together, the edges on both blades become sharper, and it makes them more efficient. This also happens in our relationships when we choose the right people to be around. That's why it's important to have a circle of good men around you. It takes a lot to be tough like iron; it takes even more toughness to be sharpened by iron.

Life experiences will generally make us more aware of what we can and can't deal with in life. One of the main things we should never tolerate in our lives is people who don't make us better. You should tolerate people who believe in you, people who encourage you to go after your dreams and goals, people who are often on the same journey with their own progress, people who hold you accountable, and, most importantly, people who challenge you. It's important in your process of becoming a good man that you have these kinds of people around you and that you communicate with them regularly. They can have a major influence on your life; in some cases, they can make or break vital points in your journey that will help you progress to the next level. Every successful person has a team around them—a team of people who are not only good for their personal brand but also good for them personally.

Don't get the two confused, because you are your business, and your business is you. Whether you work for yourself or for someone else, how you present yourself, your work ethic, and the company you keep defines you. My dad used to tell me, "If you show me a man's friend group, I can tell you where he's going to be in ten years." I was fortunate enough to have an active father in my life. I know others aren't so lucky. He has given me and continues to give me sound advice that helps me to be better in life. I wouldn't be the man I am today without his guidance and direction; he has a certain way of dropping knowledge on me that gives me chills. One of my favorites is, "Don't be the man that finds four quarters and then complains it wasn't a dollar bill," meaning the value of both is the same, but the way you get them is different. This didn't hit me till I got older. I applied this logic to my life, because sometimes we get what we asked for but not in the way we expected it. We have to be grateful for the four quarters even if it's not the dollar bill we asked for. My folks have always built me up, checked me, and helped me through anything. The true definition of people with a purpose: They always play the long game. My mother keeps me in line when I'm off the path and is quick to remind me what she expects out of me. She acts as iron sharpening iron.

One example of this is a situation that occurred when my ex-wife and I officially got divorced, and my ex asked to take one of my custody days to take the girls to a funeral. She had tried contacting me from this app we use, but my notifications were off. So, after many failed attempts at getting in touch with me, she called my mother, who is a part of my favorites on my phone, so when she calls, it gets through regardless of whether I'm on Do Not Disturb or not. When my mother called, I answered, and she said that my ex-wife had been trying to contact me about leaving to go out of town for a funeral. I texted my ex-wife back through the app. When she asked if I would give up my custody day, I initially declined because I felt it wasn't fair for me to give up my day without exchanging for one of hers. At this point, I wanted her to be somewhat fair about taking my time with the girls away from me. She fired back a reply that made me more upset and determined not to give up my time with my daughters. For several reasons, I didn't think it was necessary for them to even attend this funeral. I concluded that she could have them after my designated time and still make it to the funeral the next day.

After I sent the reply, I called my mother to inform her my ex was not willing to trade days with me or negotiate a way for me to get that time back, and without hesitating, my mom said, "No matter what she does, you need to do the right thing." I shared some words of passion, telling my mom that I wasn't going to fold on what I initially said.

Then she told me that she expected better out of me and that I should be ashamed of myself for acting like that. "You are sitting there at Barnes & Noble writing a book about how to be a good man, and you're not being a good man right now." I realized then that this was true. I had relapsed to one of my nice guy moments where I let my emotions get the best of me. I don't know about y'all, but disappointing your parents in your older age is a low feeling. My parents spent decades raising me to be better than the way I was acting in that moment. This is why it's important to have people in your corner who can see through a different lens and hold you accountable. The truth is, I had let my emotions get the best of me, and I wasn't willing to budge. But my mother was there to correct that quickly, or like rapper and activist T. I. would say, "expeditiously."

Ultimately, my mother convinced me to change my mind and let my ex-wife go to Tennessee with the kids even if it was on my custody day. I messaged her in the app and told her that she could have my day and to drive safely. I asked again if I could have the next Wednesday in exchange for her taking my custody day. She agreed to the exchange of days.

Something that was so simple was made so difficult because I wanted to be stubborn. It was God's plan for my mother to check me and let me know that I was out of pocket. At the time, I was mad at her for doing it because I wanted her to be on my side. I wanted her to justify why I was right for initially saying no, especially since she knew all the frustrations I was having with the custody litigation during the divorce process. But that's the great thing about her: She's not on the side of this person or that person—she's always on the side of what's right. This is one of the things I love so much about her, even though when it's put into action against me, it doesn't feel the best.

That's why you have to be tough and be made out of mental iron to sustain moments like this in life. This journey to being a good man is not always going to be perfect, and you won't always get it right, but it's important to have those foundational elements in place so when you do slip up, you can quickly shape up.

After the situation was resolved, I felt a sense of relief. I then began to wonder why I did that to myself. There was no reason for me to get that annoyed about her asking me for that favor. I realized after processing that I had not forgiven her for all the times she'd withheld custody from me out of anger over me not wanting to be with her. I was still holding on to some of that resentment. I decided to stop writing for the day and head back home. On my way, I stopped to get some food, and while I was waiting for my food, I started to forgive myself for how I responded earlier. I also began to forgive my ex for all the things she did to me during our divorce process. By the time my food was ready, I felt like a new person emotionally. Later that evening, my mother FaceTimed me, and we had a heart-to-heart. She was a little bit easier on me during this conversation but was still holding me accountable. I needed that more than ever. While I *wanted* to be told I was right, I *needed* to be told I was wrong, and why I was wrong. That's the difference sometimes in what we want and what we need, and how it shows up in our lives. It shows up when we least expect it during a time when we need it the most.

I'm so grateful to have moments like this to share with you. I know God has put me through so much so I can tell my story, share my testimony, and help others not make the same mistakes I did. I know I'm not perfect; I'm a very flawed man. But being a good man isn't about being perfect, it's about being good. When you aim for perfection, you often lose the purpose as to why you are doing it in the first place. Being made of iron is all about having mental endurance to move through life. Things won't always go your way, and you don't want them to. If they always go your way, then how will you ever learn to navigate through the hard times? Issues will arise—that's inevitable—but how we deal with them is what's important and most often determines more of the outcome than anything else. We have to be able to openly and gracefully take criticism and apply it to our lives.

One of the hardest parts about having people around you who can hold you accountable and correct you is being able to accept it while also using it to become better. I could have easily shut down after my mother challenged me. I could have acted like a little boy and played the victim. I choose not to do that because the only way for me to get better as a man is for me to take constructive criticism. We've all seen those people who are not teachable or coachable—they don't go far in life. I know that for a fact from my former students. The ones who were able to take advice and criticism had a different outlook on life. They saw it as an opportunity to get better rather than using it as a reason to stop trying.

BE A GOOD MAN, NOT A NICE GUY

I don't want you to get hung up on always being right. Sometimes you will be wrong, and you will learn from it. The main takeaway is to think with purpose, process with purpose, and act with purpose. I have faced many crossroads in my life, such as the one I mentioned in this chapter. I will continue to experience many more. Sometimes we are quick to react because that's how we operate as humans, but there's nothing wrong with taking a second to breathe before responding. This is also a great time for you to think about the times when you knew you were wrong, and you had people not only back you up but also support your wrongdoings. When this occurs, you may need to reevaluate that relationship along with the priority it has in your life. Relationship roles in our life change with circumstances. Our job as good men is to be aware of this and to monitor, assess, and adjust to make our foundational elements firmer and more consistent in our lives.

CHAPTER 8

NICE GUYS FINISH LAST

I KNOW THIS CHAPTER WILL BE TRIGGERING FOR some of you reading it. You will begin to realize why you have had so many failed relationships and why you think that being a nice guy is your victim card for people doing wrong to you. The truth is, shit happens to us all; everybody has a sob story about something in their life. While we can't change what has happened to us, we can control how we respond to it. When it comes to dating and relationships, we often hear the phrase "nice guys finish last." It's a saying that has been around for ages. I used this phrase many times throughout high school and college, usually with the implication of garnishing some sort of sympathy for my lack of advancement romantically with some women. The truth is, being nice can come off as being performative—it can be more about putting on a show to impress someone or to gain their validation than about being kind, which comes from a genuine place. On the contrary, being a good man is about using kindness to be purposeful and authentic when it comes to your actions and intentions.

A nice guy will go out of his way to do things for someone (especially a woman), showering them with compliments and gifts, often love bombing, and being overly agreeable to everything she suggests. While these things may seem good on the surface, they can also come off as insincere, as though you're trying too hard. In the long run, be more motivated to be kind instead of being nice. This can help people see that you genuinely care and have empathy because it involves thoughtful yet intentional actions that benefit others without expecting anything in return.

A good man understands that relationships are not about constantly pleasing the other person or trying to be everything they want. The relationship should be about service, how you can show up to serve. A good man is confident in himself and in his actions. He is not afraid to be authentic and show his true self, and he also understands the importance of boundaries and does not compromise his values, morals, or beliefs just to please someone else. Another key difference between nice guys and good men is their initial approach to dating. Nice guys often put all their efforts into trying to win over a woman, while good men focus on building a genuine connection. Instead of constantly trying to impress, they focus on getting to know the person and building a strong foundation. Additionally, good men are not afraid to speak up and voice their opinions. They know that it's important to have healthy communication in a relationship, and they are not afraid to express their thoughts and feelings in doing so. They also respect the opinions and

BE A GOOD MAN, NOT A NICE GUY

boundaries of others, making them easier to get along with in the long run.

A great example of why nice guys finish last can be found in the movie *The Mask*, a film featuring Jim Carrey, who plays a character named Stanley Ipkiss. Stanley is a banker who is considered a nice guy by his friends and coworkers. He stumbles upon a green mask in a body of water. When he puts on the mask, he turns into a green-faced, charismatic, well-dressed ladies' man. This man is completely different from banker Stanley. In every room he enters, he turns heads and people gravitate toward him because of his charm. There's one scene in the movie where a newspaper reporter comes into the bank to get information from Stanley about a crime that was committed. During their exchange, he recognizes her name as an alias to her blog called *Ask Peggy*. She and Stanley then realized he was the one who penned a guest post titled "Nice Guys Finish Last." In this post, Stanley talked about his failed relationships and dating experiences. He also said that women just don't like nice guys, and that's why they finish last. After their conversation ends, she looks at him very somberly, with pity in her eyes, and tells him he is such a nice guy and that any girl would be lucky to have him. She was affirming that Stanley was a nice guy based off her interaction with him. She could tell that he wasn't being his authentic self and that's why he was having trouble getting and keeping relationships. It was for that exact reason: being a nice guy.

When Stanley was the banker, he struggled with self-esteem and put up with mistreatment from his boss, coworkers, and others because he didn't feel worthy of better treatment. This lack of self-respect was visible in his character throughout the movie. He was afraid to step out of his comfort zone and take chances. The lack of confidence held him back in a lot of areas in his life, including relationships. This is something that men can relate to on some level, even though we don't have a green mask to put on to embolden us at social events. But we have tools like this book that act as the mask and help us transform into who we are meant to be. When Stanley became "The Mask," he had a lot of good man qualities and values. He became desirable because he had self-respect, confidence, and he knew his worth. He wasn't afraid to stand out and stand up for himself. Even though in the movie he was a bit cartoony when he became "The Mask," the message was clear. The symbolism of the mask was a great comparison because it was the visual representation of who we can be when we let go of the ideas of who we think society wants us to be.

One of the key aspects of the movie was when he started to exhibit some of the same behaviors from the mask while being Stanley the banker. His boss would always get on him about being late or doing something off task. Initially he would just take the mistreatment and not say much, but after he wore the mask a few times, he began to set boundaries and no longer accepted that treatment from his boss. His confidence from being in the mask started to rub off on his real-life persona.

It's important to note there is a distinct difference between being confident and being arrogant or cocky. A good man does not need to belittle others or put them down to feel good about himself. He is secure in his own worth and does not need validation from anyone else. He treats others with respect and kindness, and this is what ultimately makes him more desirable.

BE A GOOD MAN, NOT A NICE GUY

We all want to be desired. We are naturally social beings, and human connections are essential for our overall well-being. When we surround ourselves with like-minded, driven people who share similar outlooks, goals, and ambitions, we are more likely to succeed in what we're trying to accomplish. We feed off each other's energy and drive, pushing ourselves to reach new and greater heights. In a world where competition and individualism are highly valued, it can be challenging to embrace the concept of "teamwork makes the dream work." One of the many reasons why nice guys finish last is because they always have a team around them that is full of other nice guys. Imagine a world where we are constantly striving to bring out the best in ourselves and others by working and learning together. A world where we all work together with the same purpose, lifting each other up rather than tearing each other down. I know for a fact that in today's society, being a good man can come with little recognition, and that's okay. Being a good man is something to be proud of. It may not always be the easiest or most popular choice, but it's the right one to make.

So, why do nice guys finish last? This is the question that many want the answer to. I'm going to give it to you plain and simple: Nice guys are full of shit, they don't truly mean well, they are performative in their nice acts, they often lack values and principles, they are not genuine or compassionate, and they don't earn respect from people. This is usually because people can see right through their behavior and antics. People view this type of performative goodness as harmful and manipulative. True goodness comes from the heart, not from the desire for praise or recognition. Being a good man is never about impressing others or fitting into society's narrative or expectations of who you should be. It comes naturally to you because it aligns with your values, and authenticity will always be more attractive than trying to be someone you're not.

Growing up, especially during my high school and college days, I was known as the stereotypical nice guy. I was always trying to please everyone. I didn't realize that being a nice guy wasn't doing me any favors until I turned thirty-three. In fact, for years it was detrimental to my ability to have and keep romantic relationships. I was always doing things so people would recognize me as the harmless nice guy, not knowing I was really using my niceness as a form of manipulation to get praise and recognition. Even typing this sends me into a cringeworthy bout of "What the fuck were you thinking, Kelvin?" I look back at some of the things I did to gain people's approval and it truly sickens me. I was always taught to be polite and kind, to put others before myself, and treat everyone with respect. These are all great qualities to have, but I took it to the extreme. I would often say yes to everything whether it was something I wanted to do or not. I would bend over backwards to help others, even sacrificing my own mental health trying to be something I was never meant to be. I would often find myself feeling exhausted, overwhelmed, and unfulfilled.

You see, being kind is not the same as being a pushover. And unfortunately, I had to learn that the hard way on many occasions. People would not only take advantage of my kindness by asking me to do things they knew I wouldn't say no to, but I would let them because I didn't want to upset anyone or be seen as "not kind." There were times during my teaching career where teachers would ask me to make signs for them because I was an art teacher. I would get all kinds of requests from various people, and even though I was burned out from teaching, coaching, and being a father, I would still do it, and then would regret it most of the time. Little did I know, by constantly putting others ahead of me, I was actually hurting myself in the long run. It wasn't until I started to reflect on my actions in my older age and see how they were affecting my life that I realized I needed to make a change.

This was not an easy thing for me to do. It meant setting boundaries, saying no, and prioritizing my own needs and wants. But it was necessary for my own personal growth and happiness. Through this journey of self-discovery, I learned a valuable lesson: Being kind does not mean sacrificing your own well-being. It's important to take care of yourself first, before trying to please others. That doesn't make you selfish; it makes you self-aware. Now, I'm not saying you should stop being kind altogether. Kindness and empathy are important qualities to have, but it's important to find a balance and know when to say no.

In my past, being the nice guy often led me to finishing last. What I mean by that is I always felt like people, especially women I was trying to date, would consider me a last thought or option instead of being a priority. But now, by standing up for myself and not being afraid to say no, I feel more in control of my life. I no longer feel like a doormat, and I have more time and energy to focus on my own goals and aspirations. I'm a man of values, morals, and principles and I need to conduct myself as such. It does suck that I had to go through a painful, slightly agonizing divorce to realize this. What matters most is that we live a life that makes us happy. This may mean making tough decisions and standing on business at times, but it will ultimately lead us to a life of fulfillment and contentment. I'm thankful for this journey every day because now I know this is truly who I am meant to be. A man of purpose, a man of God, a man who does things because they are right and not for validation.

Being a good man often means standing up for what you believe in and treating others with respect and kindness. It means being honest and having integrity, even when it's not the most convenient option. Unfortunately, no matter what, you will come across people who confuse being a good man with performative acts of kindness. Don't worry about them. As long as you know your intentions, that's all that truly matters. You have to be confident in your own skin. You don't need to conform to anyone's definition of what they think masculinity is to be a good man. You can embrace your softer side and still be strong. You can express how you feel and still be tough. The true strength of a man lies in his ability to be vulnerable and authentic with himself.

My advice to you is to learn from my past. Don't make the same mistakes I did by always trying to please others at the expense of your own happiness. Find the balance between being kind and standing up for yourself. And remember, it's not about finishing first or last, it's about living a life that brings you joy and fulfillment. As we navigate through life, we will inevitably encounter situations where we must choose between being kind and standing up on business. It can be a difficult balance to find, but it's important that we learn how to do it in order to maintain our own happiness on this journey of becoming a good man.

So, change the narrative from "nice guys finish last" to "good men finish strong." Let's encourage and celebrate men with kindness, empathy, and authenticity instead of blaming our shortcomings on others. Let's continue to teach future generations that being a good man is something to aspire to, not something to be ashamed of. Being a good man is not about trying to fit into society's expectations or seeking validation from others. It's about being true to yourself and treating others with kindness and respect. Let's be proud of who we are and strive to make a positive impact in the world. Because at the end of the day, being a good man is not only about finishing strong; it's also about making a difference.

CHAPTER 9:

FRUSTRATED FATHER

BEING A FATHER IS SUCH A BLESSING. I HAVE BEEN able to witness what being a parent should be from my own father. My dad gave me many useful tools and examples of how to be a man. I know I wasn't the easiest kid to parent; I was often telling lies and trying to escape having to do schoolwork to play with my friends till the streetlights came on. Although I know he was so upset with me and wanted to blow a fuse a lot of times, he showed patience and would also discipline me when he needed to. I look back and realize that every time I got in trouble, the punishment was always in proportion to what I did. I was never over-punished by my parents, which I think sometimes happens when we let our emotions get the best of us and we end up taking it out on our children. Whether it be stress from work or our personal life, we can't let that distract us from rational parenting. It's easier said than done—I know that for a fact.

My father is a good man and was very hard on me when I was young so he could be softer on me when I was older. I made a lot of stupid mistakes such as speeding while driving, lying about my whereabouts, and getting bad grades. I faced consequences early for those mistakes, so when I got older, I knew not to make those certain mistakes again. The beauty about making mistakes when you're younger versus when you get older is that when you're younger there's a lot more leniency. The older you get, the less leniency you receive because people assume you should know better. This is why I move with caution in my adulthood because I know my punishments will no longer come from my parents; they will come from a courtroom. For instance, if I got into a fight in elementary school, I would be sent to the principal's office and have to deal with some kind of school consequence. If I get into a fight now, I could be charged with assault and possibly face jail time. This is why I think it's so important for boys to make mistakes early on in life. This way you can learn at a young age how your actions and reactions have consequences. I now make good decisions in my adult age because of this.

When I was younger, I used to let my emotions get the best of me more times than I would like to admit. This would cause me to get in trouble at school and at home. I had a healthy fear of my father because I knew he wasn't tolerating any misbehavior from me. Although I made continuous mistakes that drove him up the wall and he would rightly punish me for them, he also turned them into lessons to be learned. One of the most important lessons I learned from my father about parenting is that you never give up on your children. No matter how much trouble I caused, I never felt like he was giving up on me. He used to always say to me, "You don't throw the baby out with the bath water," meaning that you don't disown or give up on your children because they make mistakes. Because of this, he always showed me grace even when he was angry with me. He showed me that he loved me.

I want to be just like my father when it comes to parenting. I felt as though he, along with my mother, did such a great job raising me. I knew fatherhood would be a bit different for me once I got divorced, especially since the kids were spending more time with their mother than me. In the beginning of the divorce process, our co-parenting went fairly smoothly, but as time went on things got more difficult. Like most fathers, I was the one who primarily dished out consequences when it came to behavior issues. Because of this, a dynamic of "Dad deals with discipline" was created, which is fine when you both live under the same roof, because the kids also see you when you aren't being a disciplinarian. But when you go from seeing your kids every day to a few times a week, you don't want to spend the little bit of time you have with them passing out punishments because they were being disrespectful to their mother. This is where things would get weird for me because as much as I wanted to give out the same punishments that I would have if I still lived with their mother, I couldn't do it because it would take away from my time with my kids. During my parenting time, I didn't have any issues with the girls misbehaving or acting out so it felt disingenuous for me to discipline them for things that occurred when I wasn't around. This type of tension between their mother and me would cause us to fight instead of trying to figure out a solution to the issues.

I suggested that she start taking up a role as a disciplinarian when the girls misbehave or disrespect her during her parenting time. She didn't want that; she felt as though my role as their father was still to be that main source of discipline. The more issues that arose with our children, the more and more frustrated I would get with her inability to compromise and see the bigger picture. I remember being fueled by anger because she would make things so difficult for me when they didn't have to be. The nice guy inside caused me to find myself being petty and thinking of ways I could make her life miserable as well, but as a good man I knew that wasn't the answer to the co-parenting issues we were having.

Our co-parenting conflicts got so bad that our GAL (guardian ad litem) mandated that we start attending co-parenting counseling. The good man thing to do was to try to work out ways we could co-parent better for the sake of our kids. During some of the sessions, we were able to get resolutions from the therapist. He agreed that I should not be the only source of discipline in the girls' lives and that their mother needed to start finding ways to discipline the girls herself during her parenting time. Although we would come to resolutions in the therapy sessions, they were rarely executed on her end. After about six sessions I came to the conclusion that I could either let it bother me till my kids were old enough to make their own choices, or I could change my expectations of her and not be so bothered. I realized I would get frustrated because I was expecting her to take this as seriously as I did and follow through with the professional advice we were being given. I realized I couldn't change her actions nor how she felt about anything that occurred between us, so I decided not to let it bother me anymore.

I did often wonder why she would make our disagreements the children's problem; she would sometimes try to bring our oldest daughter into the equation of our co-parenting conflicts, and I did have a problem with that. One of the most frustrating parts about being a father in a high-conflict custody litigation is the feeling that you need to always defend yourself. I know I am a good man and great father. I would never put my kids in harm's way, and my intention is to always make them feel loved, safe, and secure with me. Unfortunately, during our litigation there was an extended period where her side of the family tried everything to get my daughters to dislike me or show less favor toward me. I am forever thankful these tactics never worked, but there were many times when I thought they were working. Although I sometimes would see my daughters' energy shift when they were around me and my ex-wife's family members were present, almost like they felt they had to pick a side. It gave me a lot of anxiety, and I hated seeing them act that way. But I remember Isaiah 54:17 (NKJV): "No weapon formed against you shall prosper."

Occasionally, I would find myself toggling between good man and nice guy during these moments. Picture the scenario of the angel on one shoulder and the devil on the other. Both are telling you how to handle the situation, and you're torn on how to respond. I felt like this most of the time during our three-year custody litigation. There were times when I wanted to be petty and stoop to her level, and then there were times when I wanted to be a better man by taking the high road and making the right choice by my kids.

One of the main requests we couldn't come to an agreement

on was relocation, which threw me for a loop because we had never discussed her moving or relocating with the kids. After two years went by, we finally were scheduled to go to mediation and settle this relocation issue to finalize the divorce. What I thought would be a fairly simple, quick process ended up leading to an almost five-hour battle full of disagreements and unresolved requests from both sides. As a father, I felt like a failure. I was too busy being tied up in a high-conflict litigation that I couldn't truly enjoy my parenting time. The more I thought about her moving away with my daughters, the more I felt backstabbed, angry, and foolish to think she wouldn't do something like this. I had so many negative emotions when it was brought up, but I had to hide all these emotions when speaking to my attorney about countering her proposal.

The nice guy in me really wanted to yell accusations and call her names. At that time, I wholeheartedly believed her intention to relocate was brought on by the negative emotions she and her family felt toward me, especially her mother. I couldn't help but think that everything her mother had wanted to do to her husband (my ex-wife's father), my ex-wife was currently doing to me. It seemed like I was living vicariously through their own dysfunction, in a way paying for what her father did to her mother as well.

Not only did I feel like I was getting an unfair chance in the divorce litigation, but it also seemed as if a game of favorites was being played within the system. I knew as a Black man going up against a white woman in the state of South Carolina, I would face some difficulty against her in this legal battle, but I didn't think it would be *that* biased toward her. Every lie she told was treated as the truth, and everything I said was ignored.

I hated always feeling like I had to combat what she was doing and saying to our kids about my family and me. The girls knew most of it was a lie or an extremely fabricated story to benefit their mother. Although I would often be filled with rage due to the plights of our hostile litigation, I always made sure to show up and be present for my kids because that's what good men do. We don't let our emotions get in the way of being there for our kids. Sometimes it seemed like the motive was to throw me off my game so that I would eventually lash out irrationally, which would solidify this false narrative of me being an "angry man." I could tell that every time she did something negative, it was intended to hurt me or anger me.

One thing I understood for a fact was that if these roles were ever reversed, and if she was on the receiving end of my foolish behavior, I would be considered a bad father. I could never behave in the same manner or release my emotions in the same way she did. If my daughters ever felt the need to call their mother for refuge because I was yelling, cursing, and throwing things around the house, I would probably lose my visitation rights for a while, or at least the guardian ad litem would take it more seriously and investigate it. But when these concerns were brought up by me with recorded evidence of my ex-wife doing it, I just got a nonchalant response from the lawyers and GAL. It made me wonder why these people even had those jobs—what was their true duty? It seemed like they were ignoring all the problems and red flags until we had our trial date, which was unfortunate for me because I was frustrated and released all my negative emotions in the gym and therapy. Of course, I would have loved to tell my daughters how manipulative their mother was, but I kept my mouth shut. I had to live by the motto "light will outshine all darkness." But that's hard to do when you're in the thick of it all. It's easy to become distracted by the negativity and the simple human urge of wanting revenge, but I knew vengeance wasn't mine; it was the Lord's.

The good man in me began to lean more on my faith in Christ. I started going to church more often while also attending Bible study every Wednesday afternoon. What I started to learn from doing this is that the people in the Bible went through similar struggles, yet they kept God first and their faith strong. I wasn't alone. I learned about the book of Job, and it really brought into perspective how blessings can come in various forms. Although I had mostly lost my nuclear family, I was looking on the bright side of things…I still have my kids. My kids are healthy, they love me, and they are growing into wonderful young women like I always knew they would. Being a good man during these frustrating times meant keeping my eyes on them and focusing my attention on being a better father rather than playing the game of word-for-word with my ex-wife. This was the best decision I ever made. I knew she wanted me to lose control, she wanted to see me unhinged, but that simply was not going to happen. As a father, not only do I take pride in my ability to remain stoic, but I also know how different the stakes are for me. I have a lot more to lose than most. The system isn't set up for me to get as many chances at redemption as their mother would; therefore, I have to act with kindness, integrity, and purpose. That purpose is to be the best father I can be, even in the overwhelming darkness of frustration.

Being a frustrated father can be exhausting on so many levels. The hardest part is knowing when to roll and when to fold. We as fathers can often feel like the world is on our shoulders.

BE A GOOD MAN, NOT A NICE GUY

The expectations of providing and also being stoic and calm in the middle of emotional chaos is enough to make us want to pop like a three-day-old pimple. Shout-out to those who hold it together for the sake of keeping the foundation solid but who understand it's okay to release and break down in our own privacy. This can help us release pent-up negative emotions so we can continue to push through our obstacles in life. That's what we do as good men. Some won't understand this process, but this is the expectation that society has put on us for centuries. Men can't be as vulnerable publicly as women and children. We are expected to be vulnerable only to an extent and in certain instances, and yes, it can come at a cost if you publicly mishandle your vulnerability. For instance, if your wife and children are freaking out because the basement is flooding from a storm surge, you cannot meet them with the same energy and equally freak out about it. You may be scared too, but you have to be the one to calm everyone else, get them to safety, defuse the situation, and handle it to the best of your ability. That is your duty as a good partner; that's how we earn respect. We must show stoicism in the midst of chaos.

I used to be upset by this notion and always preached the "double standard" and "unfairness" of it until I got older and realized why my father is so loved and respected, not only within our family but in society. Being in law enforcement taught him how to not only deescalate situations but how to deal with chaotic events in a calm manner. As a child, when I would freak out over something to my parents, I was never met with the same level of panic. I was always met with a calm spirit, which in turn helped calm my nerves as well. There's a reason why first responders are trained to handle situations calmly no matter how bad it is upon arrival. Can you imagine how much more chaotic it would be if they had the same reactions as everyone else involved? As much as we want to deny it, there is an unspoken rule and expectation that men are supposed to move with the same poise. This is a standard every good man should be okay with. The older I get, the more comfortable I am in my masculine energy and roles. I think it's important to understand why men and women are different and how special we are when we come together to accept each other for these differences rather than trying to challenge and change them.

We are losing a lot of good men to the narrative that being tough is a bad thing. We must reassure men that it's okay to be masculine the same way we reassure women it's okay to be feminine. In these modern times, we have so many children being raised by weak or absent fathers, and it truly shows. Good men help raise their kids. When you are a present and loving father, the results show tremendously in your children. I can see that my daughters are growing to be amazing women, women who will embrace their feminine energy. They will also understand their strength and beauty in being women. They will not tolerate a low-caliber partner; they will expect their partner to treat them well because of the foundation I have laid for them. They will not accept mediocrity from themselves, nor will they accept it in their careers, friendships, and love lives. They know and understand the duties of a good man in a relationship, parenting, and in society. My goal is to always set the standard high and be there for them no matter what they go through, to show them love, support, and strength so they can conquer all the obstacles life throws their way. No matter what happens, this is my duty as their father—even when I'm a frustrated father.

Good Man: Habits, Hobbies, and Happiness

Being a good man is not just about being kind and respectful to others; it also involves pursuing habits, hobbies, and happiness in your life. First and foremost, a good man is someone who has good habits. This includes being responsible, disciplined, and organized. A good man knows that his actions have consequences and, therefore, he carefully ensures that he is making the right choices. This could mean being punctual, keeping his living space clean and tidy, and staying on top of his tasks and responsibilities. With good habits, a man not only improves his own life but also positively influences those around him.

In addition to good habits, a good man is someone who has hobbies and interests outside of his work or daily routine. Hobbies allow a man to relax, unwind, and express himself in a creative way. It could be anything from playing an instrument, painting, gardening, or playing a sport. Hobbies provide a sense of fulfillment and can even lead to developing new skills. This not only makes a man more interesting but also helps to relieve stress and improve his overall well-being.

However, being a good man doesn't mean that he won't face challenges or struggles. But what sets him apart is his ability to find happiness despite the challenges. A good man knows that happiness comes from within; it is not dependent on external factors. He takes care of his mental health and surrounds himself with positive people and activities. He also knows how to find joy in the little things, whether it's spending time with loved ones, enjoying a hobby, or simply appreciating the beauty of nature. More so, being a good man also involves using discernment and being understanding toward others. A good man knows how to listen without judgment and offers support to those in need. He treats everyone with respect and kindness, regardless of their background or beliefs. This not only helps to build strong relationships but also creates a positive impact on society, which can contribute to our own happiness.

HABITS

Let's talk about habits, because we all have them. Some are good, like brushing our teeth every day, and some are not so good, like biting our nails when we're nervous. But have you ever stopped to think about the benefits good habits bring to our lives? Habits provide structure and routine. By doing something repeatedly, we create a sense of predictability in our day-to-day lives. This can be especially helpful for those who struggle with anxiety or other mental health issues. Having a set routine can provide a sense of comfort and stability for us, making it easier to navigate through life's ups and downs.

Habits also can save time and energy. Like the saying goes, work smarter not harder. How many times have you done something without even thinking about it? By turning certain actions into habits, we free up mental space and energy that can be better used for more important tasks. For example, imagine if you had to consciously think about how to tie your shoes every time you put them on. It would take up a lot of time and mental effort. Instead, tying your shoes has become second nature and can be done daily with little to no thought about the process.

Developing positive habits can also lead to improved overall health and well-being. Eating healthy, exercising regularly, and getting enough sleep are all habits we can develop that can significantly impact our physical and mental health in a positive way. By making these actions a part of our daily routine, we are setting ourselves up for a healthier and happier life. Habits also help us achieve our goals. Whether it's completing a project at work or saving money for a vacation, developing habits can make it easier to stay on track and reach our desired outcomes.

By consistently working toward our goals through daily habits, we create a sense of momentum and progress that can be extremely motivating for us. Another benefit of good habits is that they can help us break bad habits or addictions. By replacing negative routines with positive ones, we can gradually eliminate harmful behaviors from our lives. This is not an easy task, but with dedication and consistency, it is possible to make lasting changes and break free from destructive habits.

Lastly, habits can bring a sense of accomplishment and satisfaction. When we stick to a habit, whether it's going for a morning run or meditating before bed, we experience a sense of pride and fulfillment. This can boost our self-esteem, serotonin levels (which regulate our moods), and overall sense of well-being. I have noticed that when I stick to my habits, I show up better for the people in my life. I have also noticed that when I get off track from my good habits, I tend to fall into a mental funk. But learning to give myself grace is a habit I had to develop over time. I can't beat myself up if I don't accomplish all my daily habits. Like, some days I don't make it to the gym, which may be time-related or my body telling me it needs to rest. Instead of getting in a funk about it, I have gotten in the habit of replacing it with something else that fulfills me. This could be playing a video game, reading, or even doing some devotional work. Of course, not all habits are going to be consistently beneficial to us. They will change over time, and it's important to recognize when a habit is no longer serving us so we can be intentional about changing it.

HOBBIES

Hobbies are often seen as a fun way to pass the time, but they actually offer a variety of benefits that can positively impact our lives. Whether it's painting, dancing, or playing an instrument, engaging in a hobby can bring joy and enrichment to our daily routine. One of the top advantages of hobbies is they allow us to take a break from the stress and demands in our daily lives. In today's fast-paced world, we are constantly bombarded with work and responsibilities, leaving little time for ourselves. Hobbies provide an escape from this hectic schedule and give us the opportunity to do something we truly enjoy. It can be considered a form of self-care that helps us relax, recharge, and rejuvenate our minds.

More so, hobbies can also be a great source of creativity and self-expression. When we engage in a hobby, we have the freedom to express ourselves without any restrictions. Whether it's through painting, writing, or cooking, hobbies allow us to tap into our imagination and let our ideas flow freely. This can be especially beneficial for those who work in highly stressful, structured, and rigid jobs, as it provides an outlet to unleash creativity. This was true for me. When I taught middle school art, I was so burned out that my hobby of creating art felt more like an extension of my job. I decided to start a fashion blog as my creative outlet. I was able to find peace in taking pictures and writing style advice for men. It was something that gave me joy and didn't feel like work. Sometimes our hobbies can earn us income on the side, which is also a plus. Our hobbies can also turn into full-time careers as well. I had no idea this hobby would lead me to this point in my life. The best part about it is that it still feels like a hobby to me.

Another advantage of having a hobby is that it can add to our current skill set. By consistently practicing and dedicating time to our hobbies, we can become more proficient in them over time. This could lead to a sense of accomplishment as we see ourselves progressing and learning new techniques. These skills can also be transferred to other areas of our lives, making us more well-rounded individuals. In addition to personal benefits, hobbies can also have a positive impact on our social lives. Participating in group hobbies such as team sports or book clubs can help us connect with like-minded individuals who share similar interests. This can lead to the development of new friendships and relationships. Even solo hobbies like knitting or gardening can help us connect with others, creating a sense of community and belonging.

Finally, engaging in a hobby can be a great stress reliever. When we are engaging in something we enjoy, our bodies release endorphins, also known as "feel-good hormones." This can help reduce anxiety and boost our mood, making us feel happier and more relaxed. Hobbies can also serve as a healthy coping mechanism for dealing with stress and negative emotions, which provides us with a productive way to release pent-up feelings. Good men have hobbies, and they understand the importance of them. They also recognize that hobbies are an integral part of our lives that offer more benefits than not.

HAPPINESS

Happiness is a feeling that everyone desires. It is a state of mind and emotion that brings joy, contentment, and satisfaction. While the pursuit of happiness may seem like a very subjective and personal goal, there are many tangible benefits to being happy.

First things first, being happy can have a significant impact on our physical health. Studies have shown that people who are happier tend to have better overall health, including a stronger immune system, lower blood pressure, and reduced risk of heart disease. This is because happiness stimulates the production of endorphins, which are chemical substances that act as natural painkillers and boost our immune system naturally. Additionally, happier individuals are more likely to engage in healthy behaviors such as exercising regularly, eating well, setting boundaries, and getting enough sleep.

Furthermore, happiness has a positive effect on our overall mental health. It reduces stress and anxiety, which can lead to serious mental health issues if left unattended. When we are happy, our brains produce hormones such as serotonin and dopamine, which are directly responsible for regulating our mood and emotions. These hormones also help us cope with negative emotions and enhance our overall emotional well-being. As a result, happy individuals tend to have a higher self-esteem along with a more positive outlook on life. Another benefit of happiness is its impact on our relationships. When we are happy, we tend to build stronger and more meaningful connections with others.

Actor, producer, and rapper Will Smith once said, "You can't make people happy in relationships. You have to be already happy, and the other person be happy as well. You bring your happiness together. You should never look for happiness in someone else." Happy people tend to be more empathetic, compassionate, and generous toward others, making them more likable and approachable. But sometimes it can do the opposite; miserable people hate to see other people happy, so it can make them want to bring you down. But when you are truly happy, you don't let that behavior steal your thunder.

Happy people are often surrounded by supportive and loving relationships, which provides a sense of belonging and fulfillment. This strong social support network also contributes to their overall happiness and well-being. Moreover, happiness can also have a positive effect on our work and/or academic performance. People who are happy tend to be more productive, motivated, and engaged in their work or studies. They also exhibit higher levels of creativity and problem-solving skills. As a result, they are more likely to achieve success and reach their goals. They also work well in group settings and projects, often being a strong contributing factor to the success of the team. Happier employees or students are more likely to have better relationships with their peers and superiors, leading to a positive work or study environment. Lastly, happiness is contagious. When we are happy, we spread positive energy while influencing those around us. This creates a ripple effect where the people we interact with also become happier, leading to a more positive and optimistic society.

As a good man, it is vital for you to create your own happiness through good habits and hobbies that fill your soul. There is nothing worse than an unhappy "Debbie Downer" type of person. You know, the one who finds the bad in everything rather than trying to find the good. These people can really drain you with their negative outlook and energy. That's why, as a good man, it's important to surround yourself with other good men. Men who see the benefit in being happy, building relationships, and working on themselves. This helps you maintain the standard you have set for yourself as well. You can find happiness in this world; all you have to do is look for it. In the words of the great singer-songwriter Bobby McFerrin, "don't worry, be happy."

CHAPTER 10:

GO TO HEALTH

WHEN IT COMES TO OUR LIFESTYLE, WE MUST come to terms with the fact that our decisions and habits play a role in our health. We have to choose between what's easy and what's hard. What I mean by that is if we choose easy now, it will be hard later, but if we choose hard now, it will be easy later. In late February 2021, I was diagnosed with type 2 diabetes. I had to come to grips with the fact that I had chosen the nice guy approach to my health, which was easy then and hard later. It was easy for me to eat fast food, drink sugary drinks, stay up late snacking and playing video games, and not being active. But because I chose that, it was hard later. I now have to constantly monitor my glucose level, watch what I eat, and exercise four to five times a week. Having type 2 diabetes isn't a death sentence but it sure is scary and provides a wake-up call. I had to make the choice that I was going to not only better my life but also get and keep myself healthy.

The story of how I got my type 2 diagnosis is quite interesting. I went to my yearly checkup at my doctor's office—they drew blood, checked my heart with an EKG, and asked me standard questions about my family history and some issues I had in the past. I thought nothing of it because I felt fine; I wasn't having any symptoms. I had always been healthy for the most part, with minimal to no health problems.

For context, my father has type 1 diabetes, and we see the same physician. My dad and I also share the same name, so I'm a second. There was some confusion with our appointments in February, and the front desk worker had accidentally scheduled our appointments at the same time on the same day. My dad and I decided to go in together and make it a bonding experience, a "kill two birds with one stone" kind of deal. As we were in the patient room talking and laughing, our doctor came in and went over our blood work together. My dad's A1C—a blood test that measures blood sugar levels—is always being monitored because of his type 1 diabetes, so when the doctor read both of our A1Cs, he read mine at 13 and my dad's at 8. He was a bit confused and started to wonder if our blood work got mixed up in the lab because we have the same name. He suggested that I redo my blood work because he wanted to make sure the vials were correctly labeled.

I went back to do the blood work. While I was in there, one of the nurses confirmed that my blood work was taken on a different day than my dad's. They sent me back into the room with my dad. He continued to wait with me in the patient's office until our doctor came back to release us. After about an hour or so, the doctor came back and confirmed that the vials weren't mixed up and that my A1C was 13. At that moment, I was officially diagnosed with type 2 diabetes. I tried to process what he had just said to me. I looked at my dad, and he told me that I was going to be all right.

It was truly a blessing that my dad was with me when I received this news. I can't imagine how I would've felt or reacted if I was alone. I was filled with shock, fear, and confusion. How could I have this? How did it happen? The doctor then started asking me if I had been feeling different over the past few months. I said no, I didn't have any of the "normal" diabetic symptoms such as frequent urination, excessive thirst, or fatigue. So this diagnosis caught me completely off guard in every way imaginable. After going over the general diagnosis with me, he started talking to me about treatment options. His main concern was getting my A1C down because the number was very high. I was prescribed Metformin and started taking it that day. I expressed the fear of not being able to live a full life, and my dad reassured me that it's something I can take care of, and that I can live a healthy life with diabetes. I just needed to make some changes in my daily life. He was right; this is my health, my body, and I have the choice to do better. Although he said all this, I still couldn't shake my anxiety over it. I started to overthink about the worst possible scenarios—my aunt had died from complications with diabetes. Knowing the seriousness of this illness was getting to me mentally; I felt like I was spiraling, going down a rabbit hole of information on the internet. I watched countless videos of people who were living with type 2 diabetes, and I began to follow some people on Instagram who had it as well.

By doing this, it helped me find new information that I didn't receive during the time of my diagnosis. Although I had to fact-check a lot of the information, it felt good to be proactive and take matters into my own hands. What sucked the most was that my wife and I were at odds and things were heating up to our divorce. I had the stress of my failing marriage, along with the worry of having type 2 diabetes. It started to feel like the world was about to crumble on me. I was looking for any kind of positivity to keep my head in a good space. I knew that if I could remain in good mental health then I could get back in good physical health soon.

Almost a month after being diagnosed, I met a diabetes education specialist. It was serendipitous how we met. My youngest daughter, Flo, was on a Little League soccer team, and Kayce was one of the teammate's moms. It was so ironic because she overheard me venting to one of the other parents about my recent diagnosis. She came over to me, introduced herself, and told me that she was a diabetes education specialist at Lexington Medical Center. She told me about the program and how to get into it. You normally have to get prescribed to go to her class by a Lexington Medical physician, but it's open the first Wednesday of every month to the general public and anyone can attend. This was my only option because my physician wasn't affiliated with Lexington Medical Center.

The following Wednesday was the class. I made sure my schedule was clear so I could attend. When I arrived, there was only one other person present, an older white guy who had just been diagnosed as well. He was a truck driver and was looking for ways to care for himself while on the road. We both shared the same intent about the class: We wanted to know what foods to avoid and what foods we should start to incorporate in our diet more. Kayce was so knowledgeable; she dispelled some of our misconceptions while also giving us medical research to back it up. She told us about how our kidneys and pancreas work while having diabetes, and what to do if our glucose levels get too low or too high. The amount of information was overwhelming but in a good way. I brought a notebook to take notes, but she had everything printed out. This helped me focus all my attention on the examples she had, videos she showed us, and the slide show she went over. I learned a ton. For example, until I did that class, I had no idea that brown rice can be just as bad for glucose level spikes as white rice. The class lasted almost three hours. When the class was over, I had developed a strong level of confidence in my ability to take action to better my health while living with diabetes. We all know knowledge is power and having access to information like this is imperative.

Many people in low-income environments don't have access to this kind of medical information, and they also tend to live in food deserts. I started to think about how blessed I was to have access to this kind of life-saving information. At this point it was still early on for me, so only my family knew that I had diabetes. But as a public figure with an online presence, I wanted to share with my followers that I had diabetes while also taking them along on the journey of living with it. Doing this would allow me to open up about it while possibly helping others who are living with diabetes as well. Seeing a handsome, award-nominated author, model, and public speaker like myself live vibrantly with diabetes is very motivating for people. As soon as I shared the news on my Instagram page, I got so much support and messages from people who follow me who also have diabetes. They told me how impactful it was to see someone like me thrive in life while also having diabetes. I evolved my messaging on my platform to include health and wellness. I realized that I was more than just a style icon at this point; I had transformed into a public figure and could use my platform to speak out and bring awareness to diabetes.

This was great for me because I was now on the hard journey of taking care of my physical health. I had done a poor job of caring for myself physically, and as a consequence, I developed type 2 diabetes. As I mentioned earlier, nice guys want instant gratification, so I took the easy way instead of the hard way. The hard way is the good man way to approach everything in life, especially when it comes to your health and growth. Always choose hard; choose the road most people don't travel down. That's where the delayed gratification is. There's less traffic on that route and you can get to the destination that's meant for you. I should've chosen hard from the beginning. Hard is finding time to make a healthy meal instead of stopping for fast food. Hard is choosing to work out instead of plopping down on the couch and scrolling on your phone. Hard is taking the steps to better yourself instead of wallowing in negativity and self-pity. Most people don't and will not change until they reach a point where the pain of staying the same is much worse than changing. Then and only then are they faced with the ultimatum of easy now, hard later or hard now, easy later.

Now that I have it hard later, I use this as motivation to not only turn my life around and potentially reverse my type 2 diagnosis but to also help spread advice about my own personal habits to better manage my glucose levels. I now feel it is a duty for me to share this education with people. Starting to change my mindset and adapt a more positive outlook was game changing for me during my new health journey. Doing this allowed me to be in control of my health. I started to exercise regularly, and I changed my diet by reducing the amount of sugar and carbs in my meals. Within a few weeks, I started to notice a difference in how I felt, which was a wild moment for me because I thought I felt good before. But you know what they say: You don't know how bad you were feeling until you start to feel better, and that's exactly what happened with me. Some of the results I noticed were small things like having more energy and fewer cravings for unhealthy foods. Another thing I started to notice was that Metformin was making me feel terrible; I would get nauseous and often feel sick after taking it. After a month, I stopped taking it and planned to control my glucose levels with diet and exercise. I knew doing this was a risk, but I believed in my ability to holistically care for my body.

So, that's what I started to do. When I moved out and began the divorce process, I used it as time for self-reflection. For me, this was a blessing in disguise, a chance to have a new beginning filled with the opportunity to write my own story. I got on a daily schedule consisting of a slow morning, waking up around 7 a.m., having some coffee, walking my dog, then doing some type of physical activity whether it be a walk, bike ride, or weightlifting. I would alternate based on what I felt like doing. My main intention was to listen to my body and do what it was asking of me. I think we can get caught up in a false sense of reality when it comes to fitness. The false reality that we always must go extra hard in the gym or that we have to go to the gym to look a certain way. Instead, we need to focus on what makes us feel good when it comes to fitness. We have to do what's best for our bodies. I know for me running is difficult because I have extremely flat feet. So, I often bike ride for intense cardio. Weightlifting helps me relieve stress while also building strength. I highly recommend weightlifting being added to your physical activities. There are so many benefits to it if you do it correctly.

For the first time in my life, I was living alone, which was quite the transition after living with another person for so long. But I am so much happier alone. I feel as though I function a lot better on my own. I am able to move at my own pace, make my own schedule, and do things for myself without having to check in with someone. As time went on, I realized that intermittent fasting worked wonders for me. I fast every day for about twelve to fourteen hours, then I have my first meal of the day. I would switch between chicken thighs, salmon, or steak. I usually paired them with some eggs and one vegetable (typically broccoli). Food is supposed to make you feel good and energized. That's why it's so important for us to eat well. How can we be body positive but not do positive things for our bodies? Our bodies need nutrients, vitamins, and minerals to thrive. Unfortunately, some of us have been brainwashed into eating and drinking things that will eventually kill us. It's okay to have fast food every now and then; we all deserve a treat. I personally do one cheat meal every few weeks. My favorite cheat meal is from McDonald's. I get a Double Quarter Pounder® dressed like a Big Mac® with a medium fry. I change up my cheat meals though because you can get fatigue eating the same foods.

Being a good man means that you care about yourself—physically and mentally. You take steps to maintain these things by choosing hard and really leaning into yourself while making a positive impact on your life. A good man thinks about his future and how certain decisions can help or hurt him in the long run. My goal is to be here for a long time and for a good time. I want to see my daughters get married, have kids, and live prosperous lives. I want to be an active granddad who plays with his grandkids outside. It's imperative for me to take care of myself, to stay on top of my health. I choose to eat right, move my body, and go to doctors' appointments regularly. Managing my stress and workload is just as important. You must find a great work-life balance. No matter how much you work out, stress can kill. Being well-rounded during your health journey will help you develop stamina for life. We will face mental, emotional, and physical fatigue in life. Having a daily self-care schedule can help fight this. I felt a tremendous difference in my regulation of emotions and mood when I started to change my diet and work out more.

Proverbs 13:22 (NIV) says that "a good person leaves an inheritance to their children's children." This inheritance is more than just money. Teaching our children the importance of health can help them be better in ways we can't imagine. We must lead by example. What we teach our children will eventually be taught to their children. Children will do what they see more than what we tell them to do. For instance, if you constantly are negative, eat unhealthy foods, and don't clean up your space, advice to your children about being positive, eating better, and cleaning their rooms will not be as effective. Our children are a lot smarter than what we give them credit for. Just because they are young doesn't mean they are naïve. My youngest is one of the most naturally healthy eaters I've ever known; she's loved fruits and veggies since she began to eat solid foods.

I know I am blessed to have children who have some natural tendencies to do the right thing. But that doesn't mean

I can just slack off. I have to stay sharp and on my game so I can give them valuable insight on how to be better humans. If anything, they have held *me* accountable for certain things when parenting them, like when I would get too angry and begin to raise my voice. My daughters also give me words of encouragement that truly help me to keep going. This is not my children's responsibility, and they know that. They just love to show the same kind of love and care I show to them. As good men, we must continue to educate our children on the harmful effects of unhealthy practices like excessive screen time, smoking, and consuming alcohol. As your kids grow older, they will have more open and honest conversations with you about these topics. Make sure you're approachable and available when they bring these questions and concerns to you. Being a good man means maintaining good health, along with practicing healthy habits so you can lead a lifelong journey of wellness and share the fruits of your labor as knowledge passed down from one generation to the next. Leaving behind generational wealth is great, but leaving generational health is even better. Don't let that go over your head.

CHAPTER 11:

GOOD MAN, GREAT MARRIAGE

A GOOD MAN IN A MARRIAGE IS LOYAL, COMMUnicative, supportive, and disciplined. A nice guy in a marriage isn't loyal, he struggles to communicate, and his focus is on pleasing others for the benefit of his societal reputation. Being a good man is not about being the perfect partner, but more about being committed to constantly bettering oneself and the relationship.

Going through the divorce experience has made me question if I will ever want to get remarried. Since becoming single again, I've had the opportunity to be in a position where that potential could be a possibility one day. I often wonder what marriage would be like the second time around, since I view myself as a second marriage kind of guy anyway. Maybe it has to do with the fact that when I make a mistake and learn a lesson from it, I try not to repeat the same cycle. Common sense tells me that if I do repeat the same cycle, the consequences could be even worse the second time around, which leaves me at a crossroads mentally when I think about or even begin considering marriage. I'm not saying my first marriage was a mistake, but I do think I made a decision at the time that wasn't the best for me. And in the process of doing that, I learned a lot of valuable lessons about relationships, love, grace, and empathy. I know I wasn't a good man in my first marriage. I was definitely more in my nice guy era, and it showed countless times.

Being a good man is not always easy, but it's something that I strive to be every day. And when it comes to marriage, being a *good* partner is more important than being a *nice* partner. I believe that a strong and successful marriage requires effort from both parties, and I am determined to do my part in making a marriage work through any troubles that may come our way. When I think about being a good man, the first thing that comes to mind is loyalty. Loyalty to my wife, our relationship, and our commitment to each other. This means being there for her through thick and thin, and always putting our marriage as a priority. It also means being honest, transparent, and open with each other, even when it's difficult to do so.

Loyalty was one of the many things I struggled with. From my cyber affairs to lack of commitment, I often found myself in a whirlwind of emotions that I didn't know how to articulate at the time. There were things I needed from my now ex-wife that at the time I didn't know how to ask for without being shamed or feeling some kind of guilt. At one point I asked her if we could change up our sexual intimacy. When I suggested ideas, she told me I was disgusting and that she wasn't going to do that. Her response made me feel bad and ashamed, and I started questioning whether or not I was disgusting for requesting this from her.

This shame led me down a road of trying to fulfill my desires in other places. I soon was caught in a storm of online-based sexual affairs. I had women from all parts of the world wanting to have sex with me and it sparked interest in me. I was imagining what sex would be like with all these various women, and it drove me to a point of being more unsatisfied with my marriage. My extramarital sexual fantasies were getting the best of me. I felt so stuck, lost, and filled with guilt. I knew what I was doing and feeling was wrong, but at the same time it felt so right. I didn't know how to move past it; things got more complicated as time went on. I felt like I was sleeping next to a stranger. Our conversations became nonexistent. We wouldn't eat dinner together. Our communication was on life support. Every time we tried to talk about our issues, we ran into another wall and would fight more. It was one thing after another, and it was starting to feel like a never-ending downward spiral.

Communication is another key aspect of being a good man in a marriage, and I was failing at it tremendously. I learned that not being communicative can cause major issues in your relationship. When you withhold feelings or don't talk about the issues you feel in the relationship, tension grows. It does not nourish any connection or growth within the partnership. It makes it worse tenfold, but it's hard to realize that when you're in it. One of my art professors used to say, "It's hard to see the picture when you're in the frame," meaning it can be really difficult to see the negative outcome of what you're doing until you step out of it and can observe the damage you created.

As a good man I need to make sure to listen to my wife in my next marriage and really hear what she has to say, not just wait for my turn to speak so I can have the last word. I am very guilty of being the type of person who listens to rebut what was previously said instead of listening to understand. Through growth I have learned to express my thoughts and feelings in a clear and respectful manner, without resorting to blame. Understand that by keeping the lines of communication open and transparent, you will be able to work through any issues that arise and prevent them from escalating further. I wish I would've done a better job of this the first go-round. But life experiences have taught me to embrace the lessons I've learned from my bad decisions.

If I ever do decide to tie the knot again, I will work hard to ensure that it remains a happy and fulfilling partnership for both me and my wife. Every day, I will make an effort to show my love and appreciation for my partner, whether it's through small gestures or grand gestures. I will listen to her needs and support her in achieving her goals. I will communicate openly and honestly, and never take her or our relationship for granted. As the years go by, I know that our relationship will evolve and face challenges. But I am confident that we can face them together, with love and respect for each other.

Being a good husband also means being supportive of my next wife's dreams and goals. I need to be her biggest cheerleader and encourage her to pursue her passions and ambitions. I believe that in a marriage, both partners should lift each other up and help each other reach their full potential. It's not a competition; it's about supporting and complementing each other. One of the biggest challenges in any marriage is facing hardships and overcoming obstacles together. This is where being a good man is crucial. It's easy to be loving and kind when everything is going well, but it takes strength and determination to weather a storm as a team. In these moments, you need to stay focused on your shared goals and remind yourself that you're in this together, no matter what. In the words of the great comedian and actor Chris Rock, "People say relationships are hard. No, they aren't. They are hard when only one person is working on it. Two people can move a couch real easy. One person can't move it at all."

I didn't always get it right, and I made mistakes like anyone else. But I am committed to constantly improving myself as a man and a future husband. I believe that actions speak louder than words, so I will strive to show my next wife through my actions that she is loved, valued, and appreciated as often as I can. I know I will mess up, but it's more about the intention. If I know the intention behind the mistake wasn't malicious then I can meet her with grace and hopefully she can meet me with the same grace. A huge part of my journey to becoming a good man is my ability to really process what's going on. Sometimes it takes longer than I would like, but I would rather fully process the occurrence than react emotionally. When we are led by our feelings, we normally don't make the most sound choices that will benefit us long term. Never let a temporary emotion cause you to make a permanent decision. I have had to learn this the hard way many times when saying things I did not mean in the moment. Saying these things can spark further confrontation and make it worse to the point that you can't retract it.

We have to build a strong foundation of trust and understanding, and I believe that as long as we continue to prioritize our love and marriages, we can overcome any obstacles that come our way. I will also be committed to continuously bettering myself as an individual by taking accountability and responsibility for where I fall short in the relationship. I know that to be a good partner, I must first be at peace with myself. So, I will continue to recognize and work on my flaws and strive to be the best version of myself. I will be open to learning and growing, and never stop seeking ways to improve who I am. I now know that marriage is a marathon and not a sprint; it's equipped with wisdom over knowledge. Some people may ask what's the difference? It's simple. As I mentioned earlier, "knowledge is knowing a tomato is a fruit, but wisdom is knowing that you don't put it in a fruit salad."

Everything happens for a reason—I truly believe that. Big or small, it all has a place in our story. If all the events and issues that led to me getting a divorce would've never happened, then I wouldn't have been able to write this book. This book is coming from me as a way of giving advice to you based on the mistakes I've made and the experiences that have occurred in my life. Because of these trials and tribulations, I have grown to be a better man—a good man. If I wouldn't have gone through some of these situations, I would still be stuck in the same patterns that constantly left me in frustration and confusion. I do believe my journey and story can help other men grow in the right direction.

As you move toward being a good man in marriage, keep the Choluteca Bridge in mind. The Choluteca Bridge located in Honduras was intended to be so strong and stable that it could withstand natural disasters such as a hurricane. In 1998, Hurricane Mitch (a Category 5 hurricane) hit Honduras and caused the Choluteca River to make a new channel, which changed the direction of the water flow. This led the river water to flow around the bridge instead of underneath it. Although the bridge remained standing, the roads leading to and from the bridge were destroyed. This made the bridge useless to its original purpose. Similarly, in life, sometimes the bridge doesn't burn or break; sometimes the river moves. Sometimes, instead of situations breaking you or your foundation, they were meant to guide you to flow in a different direction.

The Choluteca Bridge demonstrates how even the most solid, advanced technology can't stop, prevent, or anticipate future disasters or conditions. This serves as a metaphor for us in a marriage: Know that problems that hit a solid foundational marriage can't and will not break it but will rather redirect the partnership to flow differently. Understand how adaptability is the true key to surviving any relationship in life. The original roads to and from the bridge may be destroyed and the purpose of it may seem useless, but the fact is, the bridge is still standing, and the water is still flowing. You must go with the flow of the water. Instead of going underneath the bridge, you are now going around the bridge. Instead of ignoring issues, avoiding conflict, and playing the blame game, you now talk through issues, using conflict to better your communication with one another. You work together as a team to resolve any problem you may face. That's how you adapt to change, even if it comes from a disaster.

CHAPTER 12:

FAITH OVER FEAR

IN A WORLD THAT OFTEN FEELS LIKE IT'S SPINNING out of control, it's easy for us to let fear take control of our lives. But as good men, we've got a choice to make. Do we let fear dictate the way we live, or do we choose faith instead? Now, I'm not talking about the blind faith that ignores reality. I'm talking about a deep-seated spiritual belief that we can overcome everything, accomplish anything, and that we can make a difference. Think about this: Every great achievement in history started with someone choosing faith over fear. They looked at the impossible and said, "Yeah, I know I can do that." Many of the things we have today are because someone took that leap of faith. That's the kind of choice we need more of; the choice of faith that not only changes our lives but inspires people and generations to come. The kind of faith that makes people ask, how was that even possible? But the truth is, anything is possible with faith. It's natural for us to get weary and doubt ourselves from time to time. We do it more often than not. That's why it takes a special person to achieve something special. And God wants us to choose faith over fear every time.

Faith is like a compass in life's chaotic journey. It gives direction when the path seems unclear, and strength when challenges feel overwhelming. Good men recognize that faith isn't a crutch, but a powerful tool for personal growth and community building. It's about finding purpose beyond ourselves, connecting with something greater. In a world full of uncertainty, faith offers a sense of hope, peace, and resilience. Choosing faith isn't always easy—trust me, I know. Fear is loud, fear is big, and fear is strong. It's in our faces, screaming about all the things that could go wrong. It stands over us, hovering like a dark cloud instilling negative thoughts in our minds.

But faith? Faith is that quiet voice inside saying, "You've got this." It's that ray of sunshine that comes after you've been stuck under that dark cloud of fear. It's about believing in yourself, in others, and in something bigger than us: God. When we choose faith, we're not just impacting our own lives. We're setting an example for our kids, our friends, our communities. We're showing them it's okay to be brave, to take risks, and to believe in the good outcome. Now, I'm not saying we should ignore our fears completely. Fear can be somewhat of a useful tool, keeping us alert and safe. But we can't let it paralyze us or stop us from living our best lives or going after our dreams.

Faith expands our horizons. It's like putting on a pair of glasses that lets you see potential where others see obstacles. Now, I'm not talking about blind faith or reckless abandon. It's more like informed optimism. It's looking at the facts, weighing the risks, and then choosing to believe in your ability to handle whatever comes your way. Remember, faith isn't just about big, life-altering decisions. It's in the small, everyday choices too. It's in striking up a conversation with a stranger, trying a new hobby, or even responding to an email.

So, the question is, how do we do this? How do we choose faith over fear? It starts with small steps. Maybe it's speaking up when you see something wrong. Or taking that job you've always dreamed of but were too scared to apply for. Maybe it starts with a menswear fashion blog that encourages you to put yourself out there to one day achieve your dream of being a model. It's about pushing through the discomfort and the uncertainty, and trusting that you'll come out stronger on the other side. Remember: Choosing faith doesn't mean everything will always work out perfectly; sometimes it works out imperfectly. But what matters is that it works out. Of course, you'll face challenges along the way, but meet them with courage and resilience. You'll be able to look fear in the eye and say, "Not today, Satan. God's got me."

In this life, one of the inevitable things we will have to face is negativity. It can come from all angles and from all sorts of people: our family, friends, colleagues, even strangers. And it's not always easy to deal with. But as good men, we have a responsibility to maintain our composure and handle these situations with grace and dignity. First and foremost, it's important to remember that negativity is often a reflection of the other person's inner struggles. It's not about us but about them. So, rather than taking it personally, we can choose to have empathy and understanding toward their situation. It's crucial for us to stand strong on our own beliefs, morals, and values. Especially when it comes to business, we may encounter people who try to bring us down, discredit us, or simply don't want to see us succeed. In these situations, it's important to hold on to our integrity and not let their negativity dictate or affect our progress. We can continue to work hard and prove ourselves through our dedication and good character.

It's also important not to give people power over us with their actions. It's easy to get caught up in other people's drama and let their negativity consume us. By doing so, we are allowing them to control our emotions and thoughts. Instead, we can choose to rise above it and maintain a positive mindset. This doesn't mean ignoring the situation, but rather handling it calmly and assertively. To do this, it's important to have a strong support system. Surrounding yourself with positive and supportive people can help you stay grounded and provide you with the encouragement you need to overcome the negativity. We can also seek advice and guidance from mentors, friends, or family who have faced similar situations. Lastly, it's important to practice self-awareness, self-love, and self-care. Negativity can take a toll on your mental health, so it's imperative to take time for yourself and engage in activities that bring you joy and relaxation. This can help you reset and approach the situation with a clear and positive mindset.

We all know dealing with negativity can be challenging, but as good men, we have the responsibility to handle it in a mature and respectable manner. By having empathy, standing strong on our values, not giving people power over us, surrounding ourselves with positivity, and practicing self-care, we can effectively deal with negativity and maintain our composure as good men.

BE A GOOD MAN, NOT A NICE GUY

As good men, we have a responsibility to lead by example. To show that faith is more than just religion or spirituality. It's about believing in the power of goodness, kindness, and human potential. So next time fear comes knocking, take a deep breath and choose faith. Choose to believe in yourself and in the possibility of a better tomorrow. Because when good men stand together in faith, there's nothing we can't overcome. Each time we choose faith over fear, we're flexing a muscle, getting stronger for the next challenge. When you're faced with a decision, big or small, and fear starts creeping in, take a deep breath. Recognize the fear, thank it for trying to protect you, and then gently set it aside. Understand that both fear and faith require you to believe in what's unknown. Choose faith, choose possibility, choose growth. Because on the other side of that choice? That's where the magic happens. Choosing faith over fear isn't about being fearless. It's about acknowledging the fear but still taking that step toward faith anyway.

As we conclude *Be a Good Man, Not a Nice Guy*, let's take time to remember the valuable lessons you have learned in this book. We have discussed the importance of staying true to our values, standing on our morals and being faithful to our beliefs, while not giving others power over us. We have also emphasized the significance of surrounding ourselves with like-minded people, the necessity for positivity, and the importance of taking accountability.

By remaining strong in our values, we show that we are not easily swayed by negativity, fear, or what people may think about us. As good men, we stand firm in our beliefs and do not let others define who we are or control our actions. This not only shows our strength of character but also serves as a deterrent to those who might try to bring us down. You can't enjoy the light without suffering in the dark. Use your negatives as a positive. Continue to move on, prosper in growth, and succeed in this life. Remember that being a *good man* rather than just a *nice guy* ultimately comes down to strength of character, self-respect, and integrity. A "nice guy" often performs out of a need for validation, approval, or fear of conflict, while a "good man" operates from a purpose of principles, confidence, and genuine kindness—not passive appeasement.

Here's six reminders to embody the difference:

1. **Develop Strength & Integrity**
   - Stand by your values even when it's inconvenient.
   - Keep your word—be reliable in your actions, not just your words.
   - Take responsibility for your choices, mistakes, and growth.

2. **Be Kind, But Not a Push-Over**
   - A good man is kind *because* he chooses to be, not because he seeks approval.
   - Don't let fear of rejection or confrontation make you say "yes" when you mean "no."
   - Respect others, but don't tolerate disrespect toward yourself.

3. **Lead with Confidence, Not Neediness**
   - Don't seek permission to be yourself—own your strengths and work on your weaknesses.
   - Make decisions based on what's right, not just what keeps the peace.
   - Accept that not everyone will like you, and that's okay.

4. **Build Competence & Purpose**
   - Master skills that give you independence and self-reliance.
   - Work on your physical and mental health—strength breeds confidence.
   - Chase purpose over people-pleasing; contribute to something bigger than yourself.

5. **Set Boundaries & Enforce Them**
   - Say what you mean and mean what you say—without being aggressive.
   - Don't let guilt manipulate you into things you don't want.
   - Surround yourself with people who respect and challenge you, not just those who take from you.

6. **Choose Hard Now, Easy Later**
   - Speak the truth with respect, but don't sugarcoat it to avoid discomfort.
   - Express your needs, desires, and opinions without fear of judgment.
   - Learn to handle rejection and disappointment without crumbling.

A *nice guy* wants to be liked. A *good man* wants to be respected. This book is dedicated to those men who can turn things around in their life no matter what they are faced with. The ones who are never consumed by fear, negativity, and lies. To the men out there who say to all those who stand in their way of achieving greatness, "You are no longer welcome in my life, my journey, or my thoughts." That you choose happiness as the real riches, health as the real wealth, kindness as the real strength, and a peace of mind as the real check. Because at the end of the day, we have a bigger and much better purpose in this life, and that is reaching our goal of being a good man, not a nice guy.

Forgiven Not Forsaken: A Letter to My Mom and Dad

Dear Mom and Dad,

I wanted to take a moment to express my deepest gratitude and appreciation for everything you have done for me. Thank you for always being there for me, through the ups and downs, the good times and the bad. You have truly been my rock, my support system, and my unwavering source of love and guidance. As I reflect on my life, I realize how blessed I am to have parents like you. You have shown me what it means to be selfless, kind, and compassionate. You have taught me the value of hard work and perseverance, and you instilled in me a strong moral compass to guide me through life. Without you, I would never have been able to become a good man, nor would I have been able to write this book encouraging and showing other men how to do the same. I know many people are not as lucky as I am to have such great parents like you. The evidence of that became clear to me the more I met people from different backgrounds.

I realized in high school how fortunate I was to have you both. So many of my friends' parents forced them to do things they never wanted to do. They would often berate them and make them feel unloved, useless, and like a burden. When I would share my sentiments about how amazing you were to me, my friends would often express envy and how much they wished their parents were like mine.

Mom, you are such a beautiful, strong Black woman who has given me unwavering love and devotion. You have always been my confidant, my shoulder to cry on, and my biggest cheerleader. Your unconditional love and belief in me have given me the strength to pursue my dreams and overcome any obstacles that come my way. I don't fear the word "no" because of you. You raised me to take risks and to always go after what I want in this life. No dream, no idea, and no passion has been too big for me. In fact, you would often encourage me to go farther and not to stop at a certain point. Because you pushed me, I am now able to see that anything I set my mind to can become true if I'm willing to work for it. I bet on myself constantly because of the confidence you instilled in me from an early age. I have undeniable charisma, unbeatable talent, and a work ethic like no other because of you. For that, I am so grateful. One day I will be able to repay you in ways I've always dreamed of.

Dad, you are such a stoic, personable, and sharp man. Thank you for being my role model and for showing me how to be a good man. You have not only provided for our family, but you have also been a source of wisdom and guidance in my life. You have taught me the importance of integrity, respect, and responsibility, and I am forever grateful for your guidance. You have blessed me with life advice that I carry with me every day. From your sayings of "you can do anything, but you can't do everything" to "don't be a person who finds four quarters and complains it wasn't a dollar bill," you have shown me how to really appreciate the small things in life. Watching you and Mom love each other and show up for one another has always given me hope that I too will one day find the same thing. You are a man who stands on business, and you don't falter from your morals, values, or beliefs. It's so impressive to see you in your older age now and your growth as a man. I idolize you and hope that one day before the good Lord calls my ticket that I can be a quarter of the man you are.

Together, you both have shown me what it means to have a strong and loving partnership. Your love for each other is evident in every moment, and it has taught me the true value of a healthy relationship. Thank you for setting such a positive example for me to follow in my own life. I wanted to start this letter off with some fancy Shakespeare-esque quote about gratitude and appreciation, but let's be real, we all know that wouldn't even begin to scratch the surface of my gratitude for you all. Instead, I'm going to give thanks the best way I know how to, which is just letting my heart and mind write what I feel about you.

Thank you for not giving up on me. I know I wasn't exactly the easiest child to raise. I mean, let's be honest, I was a little shit. I was so hardheaded and would often neglect what you told me to do and probably broke more things than I can count. But through it all, you never wavered in your love for me. Even when I was at my worst, you still believed in me and saw the potential in me. Thank you for always forgiving me. Lord knows I've screwed up. I've lied, I've messed up, I've disappointed you in more ways than one. But no matter what, you always forgave me and gave me the chance to make things right. And for that, I am forever grateful.

Thank you for never forsaking me. When I look back at my life, there were times when I probably deserved to be left on the side of the road like a piece of trash. But you never did that. Your love, grace, and forgiveness has always been Christlike. You often told me that your unconditional love for me means that there's nothing I can do to earn it and there's nothing I can do to lose it. You were always there, no matter what. You never turned your back on me or gave up on me, even at times when I gave up on myself. You two have shown me in so many ways what it means to be a good man. Whether it was through your words or your actions, you taught me the importance of kindness, honesty, and hard work. You showed me that it's not about the material things, but about the love and compassion we have for others. And for that, I am truly blessed.

I am thankful with a full heart for all the things you have given me. From the roof over my head, lessons you've taught me, advice you've given me, and the food on my plate to the unconditional love and support in my schooling, career, and throughout my downfalls. I could not have asked for better parents. You have given me a life full of love, laughter, and memories that I will cherish forever. As I navigate through life, I am constantly reminded of the lessons you have taught me. I am thankful for the values and beliefs you have instilled in me, and I promise to always stand by them. Your undeniable love and support have shaped me into the person I am today, and for that I am eternally grateful. So, Mom and Dad, once again, thank you. Thank you for everything. Thank you for being the best parents a boy could ask for. Thank you for being my rock, my inspiration, and my role models. I love you both more than words can express, and I promise to continue making you both proud one day at a time.

With all my love,
Your Baby Boy Who Is Now a Good Man

KELVIN C. DAVIS II

ACKNOWLEDGMENTS

Writing *Be a Good Man, Not a Nice Guy* has been both a personal journey and a public calling. This book would not exist without the experiences, conversations, struggles, and revelations that shaped its every page. This book was born from the tension between who I use to be and who I am currently becoming. This book is more than words on a page—it's a declaration, a challenge, and a healing.

First and foremost, thank you to God—for grace, for truth, and for never letting me settle for a watered-down version of myself. My faith has grown stronger over the past few years, I understand that I was not only called to write this book, but I was also called to start a movement.

To my dad, Kelvin Davis Sr. thank you for your love, your resilience, and the values you instilled in me. Your example laid the groundwork for everything I teach today. Without you there is no *Notoriously Dapper* or *Be a Good Man, Not a Nice Guy*.

To my brother Jamal, although we are cousins by blood, we are brothers by spirit, and you've been with me through it all—thank you for pushing me, supporting me, and keeping me grounded in who I truly am.

To my best friend Adam, thank you for seeing the good man in me before I fully saw him in myself. Your wisdom and honesty challenged me to be open in the best way. Thank you for holding me accountable and reminding me that the real strength comes from living your truth. Iron sharpens iron, and I'm sharper because of you. Cheers to many more years of friendship and watching your baby boy, Calvin, grow into a good man.

To my editing, marketing, and publishing family over at Turner Publishing, thank you so much for believing in *Be a Good Man, Not a Nice Guy*. Your belief in this message gave it wings. I appreciate you all for walking beside me in the process and honoring the rawness of my words.

To all the men in my life who shared your stories, trusted me with your struggles, and let me witness your transformation. Your courage to question what you were taught and your willingness to grow inspires me in everything I do—this book belongs to you too.

To the readers, followers and supporters—the ones who dared to dive deep into uncomfortable conversations. You are living proof that we are now ready for a new standard of masculinity...one that is rooted in integrity, not approval. Remember, if something in this book confronts you, frees you, or stirs something awake—that means it's working. Keep going. You're not alone.

Lastly, to the man I used to be, thank you for surviving. Also, to the younger version of myself: This book is for you. And to the man I'm still becoming—keep showing up. This is the work. This is the way. To every man who is choosing to evolve, this book is yours now. Keep it with you in times when you need to be reminded about why being a *good man* is the best option. Remember, *good men* finish strong, always and forever.

ABOUT THE AUTHOR

KELVIN DAVIS IS A MULTI-TALENTED INDIVIDUAL who is known primarily as a size-inclusive male model, motivational speaker, author, and advocate for body positivity. He gained prominence through his blog, *Notoriously Dapper*, which celebrates self-love, confidence, and style for men of all sizes. His blog, social media presence, and collaborations with major brands focuses on challenging traditional beauty standards and promoting inclusivity in the fashion industry.

Kelvin has been featured in major media outlets such as *The New York Times*, *The Daily Mail*, and *The New York Post* for his contributions to male body positivity. Through his work, Davis has become a leading voice in the body positivity movement, challenging stereotypes about masculinity, size, and fashion. His platform emphasizes the importance of mental health, self-esteem, and body acceptance for everyone, particularly men.

KELVIN DAVIS

A leading light in the body confidence movement for men, his persona offers empowerment and wisdom that contributes to building self-esteem for everyone. His first book, *Notoriously Dapper: How to be a Modern Gentleman with Manners, Style and Body Confidence*, was nominated for the 2018 NAACP Image Award.

ENDNOTES

1. HOT 97, "50 Cent wants no problem," posted by Montreality on Facebook, May 14, 2020, https://www.facebook.com/watch/?v=529488654387483.
2. Deion Sanders (@deionsanders), "Throwback. If you look good, you feel good! #CoachPrime (posted by @deionsandersjr)," Instagram, March 29, 2024, https://www.instagram.com/deionsanders/reel/C5HiZUoMidO/.
3. Nick Saban, "Next Level Growth – Nick Saban – High Achievers Don't Like Mediocre Performers," posted by Next Level Growth on YouTube, October 9, 2023, https://www.youtube.com/watch?v=2ulRxlork5M.
4. Marshawn Lynch, "Never forget this advice from Marshawn Lynch," posted by NFL on ESPN on YouTube, October 10, 2024, https://www.youtube.com/watch?v=zDGIxcEsxys.
5. Daryl Austin, "Divorce Rates Are Trickier to Pin Down than You May Think. Here's Why," *USA Today*, updated October 2, 2024, https://www.usatoday.com/story/life/health-wellness/2024/09/05/marriage-divorce-rate/74899214007/.
6. Joshua Bote, "'Get in Good Trouble, Necessary Trouble': Rep. John Lewis in His Own Words," *USA Today*, July 18, 2020, https://www.usatoday.com/story/news/

politics/2020/07/18/rep-john-lewis-most-memorable-quotes-get-good-trouble/5464148002/.

7. Keion Henderson, "When a Man Does Not Feel Appreciated..." posted by Motivation Real on YouTube, November 16, 2022, https://www.youtube.com/watch?v=JViezIN_i1I.

8. Adam K. Raymond, "The Rock Stumbles on a Perfect Slogan for His Presidential Run: 'More Poise, Less Noise,'" *Maxim*, May 19, 2017, https://www.maxim.com/news/the-rock-find-his-campaign-slogan-2017-5/.

9. Luis Caballero and Parker Whitten, "Effects of Pornography on Young Men's Expectations, Health, and Mindset," Texas Tech University Risk Intervention & Safety Education, December 16, 2021, https://www.depts.ttu.edu/rise/Old_Site/RISE_Peer_Educator_Blog/Effectsofpornonyoungmen.php.

10. David Goggins, "I Realized That Everybody is F**cked Up ~ David Goggins," posted by hustleism on YouTube, August 8, 2021, https://www.youtube.com/watch?v=xJGZci-KXwo.

11. Miles Kingston, "Heading for a Sticky End," *The Independent*, March 28, 2003, https://www.independent.co.uk/voices/columnists/miles-kington/heading-for-a-sticky-end-112674.html.

12. "The Lottery Curse: Are Lottery Winners More Likely to Declare Bankruptcy?" American Bankruptcy Institute, accessed March 27, 2025, https://www.abi.org/feed-item/the-lottery-curse-are-lottery-winners-more-likely-to-declare-bankruptcy#:~:text=Some%20sources%20go%20as%20far,end%20up%20in%20bankruptcy%20court.

13. LL Cool J, "LL Cool J Talks New Album, Ownership Vs Artistry, New School Hip Hop + More," interview by The Breakfast Club, posted by Breakfast Club Power 105.1 FM on YouTube, September 6, 2024, https://www.youtube.com/watch?v=BtvsibBnNhI.
14. "Noncommunicable Diseases," World Health Organization, accessed December 17, 2024, https://www.who.int/health-topics/noncommunicable-diseases#tab=tab_1.
15. Mayo Clinic Staff, "Exercise and Stress: Get Moving to Manage Stress," Mayo Clinic, March 26, 2025, https://www.mayoclinic.org/healthy-lifestyle/stress-management/in-depth/exercise-and-stress/art-20044469.

www.ingramcontent.com/pod-product-compliance
Lightning Source LLC
Chambersburg PA
CBHW021155160426
43194CB00007B/755